Managing Teacher Workload
Work-Life Balance and Wellbeing

Sara Bubb is an education consultant, writer and *Times Educational Supplement* columnist

Peter Earley researches and teaches in educational leadership and management.

Both work at the Institute of Education, University of London.

Managing Teacher Workload
Work-Life Balance and Wellbeing

Sara Bubb
and
Peter Earley

Paul Chapman Publishing

London · Thousand Oaks · New Delhi

© Sara Bubb and Peter Earley 2004

First published 2004

Apart from any fair dealing for the purposes of research or private study, or criticism or review, as permitted in the Copyright, Designs and Patents Act, 1988, this publication may be reproduced, stored or transmitted in any form, or by any means, only with the prior permission in writing of the publishers, or in the case of reprographic reproduction, in accordance with the terms of licences issued by the Copyright Licensing Agency. Enquiries concerning reproduction outside those terms should be sent to the publishers.

Paul Chapman Publishing
A SAGE Publications Company
1 Oliver's Yard
55 City Road
London EC1Y 1SP

SAGE Publications Inc
2455 Teller Road
Thousand Oaks, California 91320

SAGE Publications India Pvt Ltd
B-42 Panchsheel Enclave
PO Box 4109
New Delhi 110 017

Library of Congress Control Number: 2004107216

A catalogue record for this book is available from the British Library

ISBN 1 4129 0122 7
ISBN 1-4129-0123 5 (pbk)

Typeset by Pantek Arts Ltd, Maidstone, Kent
Printed in Great Britain by Cromwell Press, Trowbridge

Contents

List of figures and tables

Acknowledgements

We would like to thank all those who helped and contributed in some way to the writing of this book. We'd also like to thank all the teachers who come on our continuing professional development (CPD) and higher degree courses. They stimulate thought and help keep our feet on the ground!

Also thanks must go to Anique Laverdure for her help with the ATL project.

Most of all, we must thank our families – especially Paul, Julian, Miranda, Oliver, John and Diana, and Jackie, Amy and Jess – for their encouragement and tolerance.

Abbreviations

ATL	Association of Teachers and Lecturers
CIPD	Chartered Institute of Personnel and Development
CPD	continuing professional development
CSBM	Certificate of School Business Management
DfES	Department for Education and Skills
GTC	General Teaching Council
GTP	graduate teacher programme
HLTA	higher level teaching assistant
HMI	Her Majesty's Inspectorate
HoD	Head of Department
HSE	Health and Safety Executive
IAM	Institute of Administrative Management
ICT	information and communications technology
IEP	Individual education plan (for pupils with SEN)
IiP	Investors in People
INSET	in-service education and training
IRU	Implementation Review Unit
IWB	interactive whiteboard
KS	Key Stage
LEA	local education authority
Lig	Leadership incentive grant
LM	learning mentor
LMS	Local management of schools
LRA	learning resource assistant
LSA	learning support assistant
LSC	Learning and Skills Council
LT	Leadership team
MARRA	monitoring assessment, recording, reporting and accountability
NASUWT	National Association of Schoolmasters Union of Women Teachers
NCSL	National College for School Leadership
NCT	Non-contact time
NHSS	National Healthy School Standard
NJC	National Joint Council for Local Government Services
NPQH	National professional qualification for headship
NRT	National Remodelling Team
NVQ	national vocational qualification
NQT	newly qualified teacher
NUT	National Union of Teachers
Ofsted	Office for Standards in Education
OSR	organizational self-review

PM	Performance management
PPA	planning, preparation and administration
PSHE	personal, social and health education
PwC	PriceWaterhouseCoopers
QCA	Qualification and Curriculum Authority
QTS	Qualified Teacher Status
SAT	standard assessment task
SBM	School Business Manager
SCT	school change team
SDP	School development plan
SEN	special educational needs
SENCO	Special educational needs co-ordinator
SHA	Secondary Heads Association
SLT	Senior leadership team
SMT	senior management team
SNA	special needs assistant
STA	specialist teacher assistant
STRB	School Teachers' Review Body
TA	teaching assistant
TES	*Times Educational Supplement*
TPA	teacher's personal assistant
TSL	Teacher Support Line
TSN	Teacher Support Network
TTA	Teacher Training Agency
TUC	Trades Union Congress
UNESCO	United Nations Educational, Scientific, and Cultural Organization
VLE	virtual learning environment
WA	welfare assistant
WAMG	Workforce Agreement Monitoring Group
VRQ	vocationally relevant qualification

Preface

It is difficult to pick up a newspaper today without coming across an article or feature about education, especially one concerning teacher workload or recruitment and retention. Of course these are related and are often considered alongside the associated notions of staff wellbeing and teacher and headteacher stress. These are all big issues and ones which culminated in January 2003 when the government signed a 'historic' national agreement with the employers, headteacher associations and school workforce unions (with the notable exception of the largest teacher union, the National Union of Teachers). The agreement, which followed on from the proposals outlined in *Time for Standards* (DfES, 2002a), aims to help schools, teachers and support staff meet the challenges that lie ahead. It proposes action designed to help schools raise standards and tackle issues of workload. As the government Minister at the time said: 'we want to free up teachers' time to concentrate on what they do best – teaching'. The signatories to the agreement are acting together at a national level in the Workforce Agreement Monitoring Group to oversee the delivery of a seven-point plan designed to create time for teachers and heads to improve standards. (Further details of the various phases of the national agreement which are statutory and affect staff contracts are outlined later in the book.)

It was within this context of work intensification and increased teacher workload being very high on the political agenda that we were commissioned by the Association of Teachers and Lecturers (ATL) in the autumn of 2002 to undertake a six-month research and development project. We were invited to work with ATL teacher members to develop and trial a 'workload self-audit' – a tool that teachers could use to ascertain how many hours they were working each week and how they were using their time, with a view to considering how that time might be best used for professional purposes (teaching and learning), to enhance job satisfaction and to achieve a better work-life balance. It was our work on the self-audit that led to us to want to write this book.

There were several other factors, too, that made us feel there was a clear need for a book of this type. One of us (SB) has worked for many years with newly qualified teachers, both as a trainer and as a *Times Educational Supplement* (*TES*) agony aunt, and was very aware of the many things affecting their work – and life! – and the need to provide effective means of support to help prevent the high drop-out rate experienced within the teaching profession within the first three years of service. The other (PE) had researched and taught on various aspects of 'human resource management' and was very aware of the growing interest in such matters as staff wellbeing, stress management and the notion that some organizations were more 'toxic' than others! Also as a secondary school governor for many years, chairing the Personnel and Staff Development Committee, there was an awareness of recent high-profile stress cases with their legal implications for employers. In addition it was becoming apparent that some government initiatives such as Investors in People, Healthy Schools and the Well-Being Programme had a lot to offer schools as they increasingly focused their efforts, rightly, on their people. After all if a school is spending the vast bulk of its budget on its staff, it makes sense to ensure the 'human resources' are giving of their best and that the school and governing body is a 'good employer'. This also makes a lot of sense for those schools finding it difficult to recruit staff – after all, if you have a choice as to where to teach where would you prefer to go – a school that is concerned with your welfare or one that is not?

The need for a book dealing with all these issues was obvious we thought, but we also felt that what was needed was not so much an academic tome but rather a concise, 'teacher-friendly' guide to this burgeoning field. We wanted to provide an overview by setting the scene but we also wished, by drawing on relevant research and writing, to offer a critical eye on what's happening rather than just following the government's agenda. What, for example, is the reality of workload reform in a time of budget constraints?

Of course the reader must be the judge of how successful we have been, but hopefully we will have achieved our main aim of offering the busy practitioner an overview of what's happening in this field, along with some suggestions and advice as to how to improve matters at both individual and school level.

The book is divided into three sections. We begin by looking at *wellbeing and workload*. What do we know about teacher workload and how teachers spend their time, what are the causes and effects of excessive workload, especially in relation to wellbeing, stress and, crucially, recruitment and retention? Chapter 2 asks what is happening to help address workload and wellbeing, and gives consideration to the plans for the remodelling of the school workforce with reference to, for example, the DfES's Transforming School Workforce Pathfinder Project, the National Remodelling Team (NRT), higher level teaching assistants (HLTAs), bureaucratic burdens, the Well-Being Programme and issues surrounding staff recruitment and retention.

The second section is entitled '*How do you change it?*' and consists of three chapters, the first of which covers the crucial area of managing change. It asks why is change necessary and why managing it is so complex, particularly dealing with resistance and conflict. Models for changing workload and wellbeing are examined, including the approaches of the National Remodelling Team and the Well-Being Programme.

Chapter 4 is about auditing how teachers spend their worktime and it is here we introduce the ATL worktime audit. We explain how to complete it and outline briefly the main findings of our piloting of the audit, including how teachers were able to make more effective use of time and to bring about change in their working lives.

The following chapter – Chapter 5 – continues this theme when it provides advice and guidance on taking care of staff. We look at work-life balance, time and stress management and, generally, how to make schools better places in which to work.

The third and final section provides *ideas for the different groups* working in schools – teachers, support staff and school leaders (heads, deputies, middle managers). Chapter 6 examines how teachers can save time by looking at the big time-consumers such as planning. It also considers marking, report writing, display and working with teaching assistants. The latter topic is given further consideration in the next chapter which discusses how support staff can be effectively deployed in schools. Paraprofessionals who teach and cover, including teaching assistants and HLTAs, are discussed along with staff in pastoral and administrative roles. Forms of organizational support provided by bursars and premises managers are also examined. The chapter concludes by considering a number of unresolved issues relating to support staff, such as whether an increase in support staff will mean fewer jobs for teachers, and whether we are just shifting stress and long working hours onto other people. Are we exploiting support staff and is teacher workload being reduced at their expense? We know, for example, that support staff earn significantly less than their professional colleagues.

In the final chapter consideration is given to school leaders who play a crucial role in staff wellbeing and workload – including their own! We focus on what is known about effective leadership and management in this area, and highlight some of the key skills which may need developing, such as meetings management, delegation and communication skills. School leaders and managers through their actions can help ensure the school as a workplace is relatively 'stress free' and that the workload and wellbeing of others is given the importance it deserves. However, there is also a need for their own wellbeing to be given high priority, something we argue that does not always happen as some heads and other school leaders take on more – not less – responsibility and workload! The wellbeing of school leaders, indeed all staff, is crucial to an effective school and it is hoped that this short book will be used to ensure that the school's most important resource is empowered and enabled to do its job well – which, of course, is to ensure the quality of education offered to its pupils is second to none!

Section A

Wellbeing and workload

Chapter 1

What do we know about teacher workload and wellbeing?

- Teacher workload
- Wellbeing
- Recruitment and retention

If, as the well-known education commentator Michael Fullan (2003) suggests, leadership is to this decade what standards based reform was to the 1990s, then staff workload and wellbeing – the subject of this book – can be seen as linking the two. It is now generally recognized that 'people matter' and, as we have argued elsewhere (Earley and Bubb, 2004), successful education reform and enhancing the quality of teaching and learning depend heavily on well-trained, developed and valued 'human resources'. If schools are to continue to improve, then urgent and ongoing attention must be given by school leaders to their main resource – their people. In this chapter, we set the context in which workload, wellbeing and related issues such as staff recruitment and retention have come centre stage. We give a brief overview of the many studies investigating these critical areas and outline their main findings.

TEACHER WORKLOAD

Over the last five years or so there has been mounting concern over teacher workload and the associated problems of health, wellbeing, recruitment and retention. Teachers need time to reflect on their work, plan lessons, develop skills and knowledge, and interact with colleagues. The government is committed to achieving significant reductions in teacher workload and yet at the same time to raising standards and achieving improvements in the quality of teaching and learning. In October 2002 the (then) Secretary of State, Estelle Morris, said:

A tired teacher is not an effective teacher. Nor is that teacher allowed to focus on what is most important – teaching. Teachers on average are expected to spend some 20 per cent of their time on non-teaching tasks that other adults could do just as well instead.

(DfES, 2002a)

Average working week

But what is the actual picture on workload? The scale of the problem of teacher workload has been outlined by studies conducted for the government by PriceWaterhouseCoopers (PwC, 2001), the School Teachers' Review Body (STRB, 2000; 2003) and, more recently, by the University of Birmingham (Thomas et al., 2004). The sets of findings on worktime make for interesting reading. Figure 1.1 and Tables 1.1 and 1.2 show the findings from the three studies that, reassuringly, demonstrate broadly similar pictures on workload.

Figure 1.1   **Average hours worked by full-time teachers in a week in March 2003**

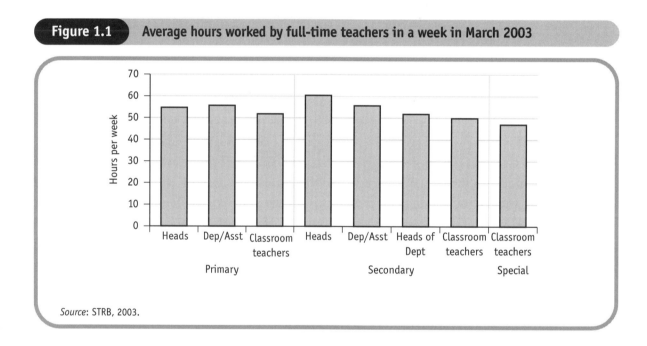

Source: STRB, 2003.

The School Teachers' Review Body figures for 2003, based on 2,694 teachers' diaries for a week in March, show the average hours worked for headteachers, deputy heads and classroom teachers (see Figure 1.1). The figures are similar to those recorded in the PwC study two years earlier and the University of Birmingham data collected in 2002, as can be seen in Table 1.1. Findings from the University of Birmingham's evaluation of the Pathfinders project (Thomas et al., 2003) found teachers working an average of 53.9 hours in primary and 50.8 hours in secondary, with heads spending 57.6 (primary) and 58.8 (secondary) hours. However, averages disguise a wide variation. For instance, the STRB data found that, although primary teachers on average work some 52 hours in term time, 16 per cent work over 60 hours and around 6 per cent under 40 hours.

Table 1.1	Teacher workload study (Thomas et al., 2003)

Occupation	Average weekly hours		Average total holiday hours		Total annual hours	
	STRB 2000	UoB 2002	PWC 2001	UoB 2002	STRB/PWC	UoB 2002
Primary schools						
Headteachers	58.9	57.6	122.4	139.4	2,420	2,386
Deputy heads (1)	56.2	56.8	115.5	137.1	2,307	2,352
Classroom Teachers (2)	52.8	53.9	97.4	114.0	2,157	2,216
Secondary schools						
Headteachers	60.8	58.8	155.5	163.7	2,527	2,457
Deputy heads (1)	58.6	55.9	149.6	138.0	2,435	2,318
Heads of faculty (3)	52.9	51.7	149.6	121.1	2,213	2,137
Classroom Teachers (4)	51.3	50.8	113.3	110.5	2,114	2,092
Special schools						
Classroom Teachers (2)	51.2	52.8	130.8	126.0	2,128	2,185
National averages for other managers and professionals						
All managers (ONS)	46.3		0		2,222	
All professionals (ONS)	44.0		0		2,112	

Notes:

(1) All leadership group except head teacher (deputy, assistant head, leadership group)

(2) All other teachers, excluding trainees

(3) Management points, recruitment and retention points, advanced skills teachers

(4) NQTs, main scale, upper scale

ONS = Office of National Statistics

Table 1.2	Comparing the hours worked by teachers in a week in March 1994, 1996, 2000 and 2003 (STRB, 2003)

	Total average hours			
	1994	1996	2000	2003
Primary				
Headteachers	55.4	55.7	58.9	55.5
Deputy/assistant heads	52.4	54.5	56.2	56.4
Classroom teachers	48.8	50.8	52.8	51.8
Secondary				
Headteachers	61.1	61.7	60.8	60.9
Deputy/assistant heads	56.9	56.5	58.6	56.5
Heads of faculty/department	50.7	53.0	52.9	52.7
Classroom teachers	48.9	50.3	51.3	50.8
Special (a)				
Classroom teachers	47.5	50.0	51.2	47.6

Notes:

(a) Heads and deputies/assistants omitted because of low sample numbers.

Interestingly, the most recent School Teachers' Review Body report (STRB, 2003) shows that workload, expressed in terms of the average number of hours worked in a week in term time, has declined slightly since the previous survey in 2000, as can be seen in Table 1.2. (This table compares results from surveys of the same week in March in 1994, 1996, 2000 and 2003.) The average length of primary teachers' weeks has dropped from 52.8 to 51.8 hours, and for secondary from 51.3 to 50.8 hours. For teachers in primary schools, there is a broad pattern of average total hours worked reducing with higher levels of classroom support. The figures for primary deputies have gone up slightly (by 0.2 hours) but down for their secondary counterparts (by 2.1 hours). The greatest reduction in working time was experienced by primary headteachers – from 58.9 hours in 2000 to 55.5 hours in 2003. This was the only difference that was found to be statistically significant (STRB, 2003, p. 3).

Perhaps surprisingly, no strong pattern emerges in the average hours worked by teachers in schools with different numbers of pupils with special needs or with different degrees of social deprivation. In the secondary sector, the STRB survey found that people who teach English work the longest weeks:

- English teachers' term time working week – 52.2 hours
- Maths teachers' term time working week – 50.6 hours
- Science teachers' term time working week – 51.0 hours.

Outside the working day

The PriceWaterhouseCoopers research in 2001 found that teachers' working weeks were more intensive than other professionals and that holiday working was widespread, as can be seen in Table 1.1. However, if you spread teachers' hours across the year they are not dissimilar to other UK professionals. But one needs to take account of the intensity and performance nature of teaching. It is very tiring. As a job it has many similarities to acting, but no one would expect an actor to do be on stage for five hours a day, five days a week and 39 weeks a year.

About a quarter of teachers' term time work happens well outside the standard nine till five day. Primary teachers do between 7 and 9 per cent of their work at weekends. In secondary schools, the average falls between 8 and 11 per cent. A further 14 to 17 per cent of work in primary schools and 15 to 18 per cent of work in secondary schools is carried out after 6.00 p.m. or before school starts, on weekdays.

Nearly two-thirds (63 per cent) of evening and weekend work by full-time primary classroom teachers is spent on lesson preparation, marking etc., with over half of this time spent on planning lessons and most of the rest on marking. For secondary teachers, the equivalent figure is 70 per cent, with the vast majority of this time split equally between planning and marking.

How teachers spend their time

The School Teachers' Review Body breaks the job of teaching down into these headings:

- Teaching

- Lesson preparation, marking

- Non-teaching contact with pupils and parents

- School/staff management

- Administrative tasks

- Individual/professional development.

We examine these and each category's subheadings in Chapter 4 when we discuss the ATL teacher workload audit. Table 1.3 shows how much time teachers spend on each of these aspects in a week. Classroom teachers spend less than two-fifths of their time teaching – 36 per cent in primary and 39 per cent in secondary schools. Although secondary teachers spend less time teaching their own lessons, they spend more time covering for teacher absence and teaching outside the timetabled day. Primary teachers spend a quarter of their time on preparation and marking. For secondary teachers, the figure is higher, with nearly one-third of their time dedicated to these activities. They spend less time planning and preparing lessons but spend more time marking pupil work and writing reports. The average hours spent on general administrative tasks are higher in primary (12 per cent) than in secondary schools (7 per cent of total time).

Table 1.3   **Average hours worked by full-time classroom teachers (STRB, 2003)**

	Average hours		Percentage of total	
	Primary	Secondary	Primary	Secondary
Total	51.8	50.8	100	100
On grouped activities				
Teaching	18.6	19.6	36	39
Lesson preparation, marking	12.9	14.8	25	29
Non-teaching contact	5.8	6.7	11	13
School/staff management	3.9	2.9	8	6
General admin. tasks	6.1	3.6	12	7
Individual/professional	3.2	2.2	6	4
Other activities	1.2	1.1	2	2

Independent schools

Workload is as much of an issue in the independent sector as it is in state schools. A survey of 300 ATL members in independent schools in March 2004 found that:

- 85 per cent of the teachers surveyed said that their excessive workloads were having a detrimental impact on their home life

- 60 per cent worked more than 50 hours a week

- 35 per cent said their excessive workload left them feeling exhausted and stressed on a daily basis

- 30 per cent stated that they had no time for a social life

- 64 per cent were expected to perform tasks they felt shouldn't have to be carried out by a teacher.

The majority of the teachers surveyed said the pressures of work left them with no time to join in with any family activities during term time, which often led to arguments and resentment within the family. A 46-year-old English teacher at a boys' independent school spoke of how his unpredictable teaching hours and additional duties left him with no spare time. He said:

> I often don't know what my finishing time will be, as sometimes at short notice I am expected to teach the under-14 rugby team after school, as the school's PE teacher is employed only on a part-time basis. This results in me not getting home until mid-evening. By then, I don't have the time and energy to do any non-work-related activities other than eating and sleeping. I'm also too tired to have a social life.

(ATL, 2004).

Causes of excessive workload

The PriceWaterhouseCoopers (2001) and STRB studies' findings and recommendations were important and led, indirectly, to the DfES-funded pathfinder pilot study (in 32 schools), the government's remodelling agenda, and the 'historic' agreement with the school workforce unions about reforming the workforce. The PwC report noted that teachers perceived a lack of control and ownership over their work, undertaking many tasks, particularly documentation, which were not seen as supporting learning. It also noted that teachers felt that 'the pace and manner of change was working against achieving high standards and that they were insufficiently supported to meet these changes and were not accorded the professional trust that they merited' (PwC, 2001, p. 1).

The evaluation of the pathfinder pilot projects also sought to understand the causes of excessive workload. Thomas et al. (2003) found that teachers pointed to five main reasons. The most popular was non-teaching tasks, e.g. photocopying, filing, money collection, acting as a social worker, paperwork, form filling, duplicating information and typing letters. Linked to these concerns was the volume of work that had to be taken home and the culture of high expectations in some schools.

The second reason was MARRA (monitoring, assessment, recording, reporting and accountability) with views including: lack of time to do this; overburdened by the amount to do; unnecessary components of this work; and marking coursework. These issues were also reflected in comments on the negative aspects of increased accountability.

The third reason was covering lessons for absent colleagues and the loss of non-class contact time. These were reflected in teachers' comments such as: teaching too many classes; lack of non-contact time; too many supervisions and duties; covering for staff absences; teaching timetable too full. The curriculum and the organization of pupils were issues that were raised most in the primary schools. Government/school initiatives were the fourth reason identified for high workload by the pathfinder evaluators. There were too many initiatives and these were too time-consuming and created overload. There was constant change and a lack of co-ordination of initiatives.

The fifth set of reasons was planning: poor planning within the school/department; lack of time set aside for planning; plans that were produced were ineffective for their purpose; duplication of planning information; lesson planning; and target setting. Embodied here were comments from teachers about the problems of prioritizing multiple and competing demands. There was a difficulty in achieving a balance between teaching and administration – and evidence of a growing level of dissatisfaction at not being able to complete work (Thomas et al., 2003).

Effects of working long hours

The Chartered Institute of Personnel and Development (CIPD, 2001) has written about the effect of working long hours. This found that one in three partners of people who work more than 48 hours in a typical week say that the time the 'long hours' worker spends at work has an entirely negative effect on their personal relationship. Seventy per cent of partners interviewed by the CIPD reported that the 'long hours' worker is sometimes too tired to hold a conversation and just over 40 per cent agreed that they were fed up with having to shoulder most of the domestic burden.

Most 'long hours' workers themselves felt that they have struck the wrong work-life balance, with over one-half (56 per cent) saying that they have dedicated too much of their life to work. Two-fifths of those working more than 48 hours per week reported that working long hours had resulted in arguments with their spouse or partner in the last year and the same proportion felt guilty that they were failing to pull their weight on the domestic front. More than a quarter of partners with children of school age or younger say that the time the 'long hours' worker spends at work has a negative effect on their relationship with their children.

The government is determined to tackle this agenda of long hours working and work-life balance. Its response, outlined later in the next chapter involves remodelling or reforming the school workforce (DfES, 2002a), and is presenting a considerable challenge to school leaders and the professional associations and unions. But workload and work-life balance are closely aligned to wellbeing, and the wellbeing of teachers (and other staff) today affects the wellbeing of society tomorrow.

WELLBEING

Unless the wellbeing of individual teachers and the profession as a whole is improved, the standards of education and the educational experience of young people will suffer. As Mike Finlayson, of Teacher Support Scotland, has noted:

We are not talking here about stress management, exercise regimes, giving up smoking or improving diets: we are talking about the physical and emotional wellbeing of a profession that faces considerable and unique pressure: a profession that shapes the society of the future and indeed, the nation's future wealth, in all its guises.

(2002)

Stress and absence

Teachers suffer greater levels of stress than comparable occupational groups but their levels of absence from work are lower. Department for Education and Skills statistics show that 57 per cent of teachers (293,000) took time off sick in 2002 – a total of 2.75 million days were taken in sickness absence compared to 2.5 million in 1999. A CIPD report found that public sector employees had higher absence levels (4.6 per cent) than workers in the private sector (3.1 per cent) with teachers averaging 4.2 days off per year compared with the health, police and fire services at five days (CIPD, 2003). However, teachers do work a shorter year than most workers. Older teachers are absent more frequently than younger ones and the most common causes of absence are minor illnesses (such as colds and flu) with stress-related absence being the fourth most frequent reason.

The Teacher Support Network (TSN, 2002) considers that many schools are suffering from institutional stress. There are a number of issues inherent in work organizations that are stressful, for example:

- Poor workplace environments

- Excessive working time and workload

- Lack of personal fulfilment and poor career prospects

- Internal politics

- Excessive bureaucracy

- Poor communication

- Low morale

- Resistance to change or excessive change

- A blame culture (TSN, 2002).

All the above issues apply to workplaces up and down the country, but they are especially appropriate to schools. What's even worse is that teachers perceive additional pressures, such as:

- Low public esteem

- Increasingly difficult parent and students

- Comparatively poor financial rewards

- Ofsted inspections

- Lack of control over their job.

The Health and Safety Executive (HSE) estimate that around 40 million working days are lost in the UK each year as a result of stress-related illness and that up to 60 per cent of all absences from work are caused by stress (HSE, 1995). The HSE sees a clear link between poor work organization and subsequent ill health: about half a million people in the UK experience work-related stress at a level that they believe is making them ill (HSE, 2003; Willson, 2004). Attributing absence and illness to stress is not always easy but a Health and Safety Executive report in 2000 put teachers at the top of the stress league. In a survey of 17,000 people, it found that 41.5 per cent of teachers reported high stress, followed by nurses (32 per cent) and managers (28 per cent).

Regulations introduced in 1999 have made employers legally responsible for assessing the health and safety risks of their employees, including stress. Perhaps unsurprisingly, a recent Trades Union Congress (TUC) survey found that stress was the main health and safety concern in four out of five schools. An analysis of the first four years of the telephone helpline – Teacher Support Line (TSL) – found that over 10 per cent of calls from teachers were about depression, anxiety and stress-related sickness. It counsels, on average, 19,000 teachers per year or 4.3 per cent of the profession. Ten per cent of calls were about conflict in the workplace and about 5 per cent about workload concerns (Lepkowska, 2004a).

Evidence about stress amongst the teaching profession is also found in the Northern Ireland Teachers' *Health & Wellbeing Survey* conducted in 2001. This involved an anonymous self-completion questionnaire, sent to nearly 24,000 heads and teachers, with a response rate of 50 per cent. The report notes that the main causes of job-related stress reported were 'having too much work to do' and 'too much administration/paperwork'. Sixty-two per cent of respondents also reported that 'lack of time to prepare lessons' was a cause of unwanted stress. Other findings were:

- 27 per cent felt that they were not able to cope with the stresses of the job.

- 66 per cent stated that job-related stress impacted on their lives outside work to some or a large extent.

- 17 per cent reported that non-job-related stress impacted on their work to some or a large extent.

- 15 per cent of teachers were absent from school in the last year due to job-related stress.

- 12 per cent were absent due to non-work-related stress.

- On average teachers who were absent due to job-related stress were absent for 14 days in the last year.

- Of those who were absent due to non-job-related stress the average number of days absent was 9.5 days.

- Those who reported that they found their job very or extremely stressful also reported lower levels of job satisfaction.

With significant numbers of staff within the UK reporting high levels of stress it is apparent that work around the wellbeing of the school's most important resource – its people – is long overdue. And of course there are implications for managers. As Dunham notes: 'There is often an inverse relationship between management skills and staff stress: good management brings less stress but poor management results in more stress' (1995, p. 141).

RECRUITMENT AND RETENTION

Recruitment of teachers has become increasingly difficult, a point made in a recent Audit Commission (2002) report into public sector employment and by the United Nations Educational, Scientific and Cultural Organization (UNESCO), which suggests an international crisis. Teacher recruitment and retention is a national concern in England; this reflects a wider global unease about teacher supply (McGraw, 2001) as well as the burgeoning problem of hard-to-staff schools in large conurbations such as London. Recent research suggests that the teaching profession is not renewing itself and teacher shortage is becoming endemic (Horne, 2001; Smithers and Robinson, 2001).

Recruitment and retention are affected by a range of factors. For example, a recent study of teachers' experience and attitudes carried out by Demos, suggests that low pay, increasing workload and stressful conditions are only part of a complex set of factors contributing to the acute recruitment and retention problems the profession is facing. According to this research, lack of professional autonomy and inflexible working patterns also contribute to the relative unattractiveness of teaching (Horne, 2001).

Liverpool University's Centre for Education and Employment Research carried out an independent study for the National Union of Teachers that identifies workload, pupil behaviour, constant and imposed change, and salary levels as key issues relating to recruitment and retention (Smithers and Robinson, 2001). A study by the same team commissioned by the DfES to investigate the factors affecting teachers' decisions to leave the profession during the calendar year 2002, found they were influenced by five main considerations: workload, new challenge, the school situation, salary and personal circumstances (Smithers and Robinson, 2003). Of these factors workload was by far the most important, and salary the least. The researchers found that the leavers from the teaching profession tended to be disproportionately the young with a few years service or older teachers approaching retirement. A systematic review of research on recruitment and retention in initial teacher training has identified that those entering teaching do so mainly for intrinsic reasons, though extrinsic factors play a part (Edmonds et al., 2002).

A silver lining of this generally gloomy picture is that competition for recruitment between schools, local authorities and, even, countries is likely to be a driver to improve working environments for teachers and other staff. Teachers are already making choices about where they wish to live and work, and increasingly take into account working conditions, including the attitude of the employer and their practices in relation to the health and wellbeing of staff. Unless teaching is perceived to be a rewarding and less stressful career, there can be little doubt that recruitment in the future will continue to be a major challenge. As Totterdell et al. (2002) have argued, the impact a school can make by self-consciously and self-critically orchestrating a positive staff retention strategy should not be underestimated. They also argue that teachers contribute fundamentally to the quality of society and to its future wellbeing, stating that if we want to recruit and retain high-quality entrants to the profession, then, as the Audit Commission (2002) has suggested, like other public sector workers, their 'work experience must match ... expectations; the working environment must engage, enable and support staff and they ... should feel valued, respected and rewarded' (p. 4).

CONCLUSION

From a financial perspective, the cost of high staff turnover, sickness, stress-related illness and early retirement is substantial and a drain on resources. Young people now joining the profession have a different attitude to work and are less willing to put up with poor management and unenlightened employers who can only see them as 'human resources'.

'Good' employers have long recognized the value and cost-effectiveness of providing support to their staff. As Finlayson (2002) notes they are: 'very aware that the health and wellbeing of teachers indirectly affects their recruitment and retention, sickness and absence rates, levels of early retirement, quality and standards of teaching and ultimately the educational experience and emotional wellbeing of young people'.

Schools that don't look after their staff usually lose their best people. The arguments for giving staff the care and attention they deserve, including their training and professional development and a proper work-life balance are clear. To conclude we believe that a focus on staff wellbeing:

- helps everyone be more effective in their jobs, so pupils learn and behave better and achieve higher standards

- improves retention and recruitment – word gets around about the places where you're looked after, and where you're not

- contributes to a positive ethos where people feel valued and motivated

- makes for a learning community – the pupils are learning and so are the staff

- is a professional entitlement

- saves money – the costs of recruiting and inducting a new teacher into a school can be about £4,000.

If the expertise and experience of staff is increasingly seen as a school's most precious resource, then the management and leadership of people and their development and wellbeing must be seen as an integral part of managing the total resources available to the school (Earley and Bubb, 2004, p. 2). Better retention rates, improved staff morale, greater control and ownership, and school managers better equipped to respond to demands for change can only assist in the drive for school improvement.

There are things that school leaders and managers can do to prevent and control work-related stress – and of course the law now requires us to take action. But wellbeing is much more than about stress and its alleviation. As Finlayson (2002) notes, school support is not just dealing with the symptoms or sending staff on stress management courses, rather it is:

> an ethos and management culture that recognises the particular needs of teachers and supports them. It is about individual development, especially management competency and leadership. Poor management and leadership are detrimental to the wellbeing of staff. It is about school-centric initiatives that improve wellbeing in the school community. It is about policies and practices that consider individual and organisational wellbeing. It is also about helping teachers to take responsibility for their own health and wellbeing. It is about changing the perceptions, of employers, parents, students, the public and of teachers themselves.

In the next chapter we consider the response to this state of affairs by examining various initiatives and schemes, many government-led, that are currently available for schools to consider in their attempts to tackle workload and wellbeing, issues which schools ignore at their peril.

Chapter 2

What's happening to help address workload and wellbeing?

- Remodelling the school workforce
- What help is there?
- Staff wellbeing
- Recruitment and retention

The previous chapter gave a brief overview of the context and background concerning the main areas around workload and wellbeing. This chapter considers the same areas – teacher workload, remodelling or reforming the school workforce, staff wellbeing, and recruitment and retention – to provide a synopsis of the main developments happening on the ground. It asks what work is taking place in relation to these key areas, so that you know what schools and local educational authorities (LEAs) are doing and what help is currently available to you. It begins by considering the related areas of teacher workload and the remodelling of the workforce.

REMODELLING THE SCHOOL WORKFORCE

In May 2002 the School Teachers' Review Body (STRB) published its *Special Review of Approaches to Reducing Teacher Workload*, which built on the PriceWaterhouseCoopers (2001) workload study and responded to issues raised by the then Secretary of State, Estelle Morris, in a pamphlet, *Professionalism and Trust*, published by the Social Market Foundation in 2001. The government published its formal response to the STRB workload review, along with proposals for radical reform of the school workforce. This was called *Time for Standards* (DfES, 2002a) which updated the policy framework for England on school workforce remodelling, and provided an overview of the response to the STRB (including the proposals for consultation) and the other documents:

● *Developing the Role of School Support Staff – a Consultation Paper for England (DfES 2002b)*

● *Draft Regulations to be made under Section 133 of the Education Act 2002*

● *Guidance on Planning for Primary Teachers in England – Developed with Ofsted and the QCA to help teachers reduce unnecessary documentation when planning. (DfES 2002a)*

This was followed in January 2003 with the signing of a national agreement – at the time described by the government as 'historic' – between government, employers and (the majority) of school workforce unions to help schools, teachers and support staff meet the challenges that lay ahead. 'It promises joint action, designed to help every school across the country to raise standards and tackle workload issues' (DfES 2003a, p.1).

Remodelling is 'an opportunity to reassess the work and role of everyone involved in educating young people. Remodelling is not a "nice to do" it's a "must do"' (NRT website). Schools are under pressure to raise standards and tackle workload, while at the same time having to deal with a number of unavoidable issues:

● Workload is the major reason cited by teachers for leaving the profession.

● Over 30 per cent of a teacher's working week is spent on non-teaching activities.

● Teachers generally have a poor work-life balance.

● 45 per cent of teachers are due to retire within the next 15 years.

● One in five new teachers leave the profession before they reach their fourth year of teaching.

● There is a need for development of professional support staff.

● There are specific teacher shortages in a number of key subjects (NRT website).

● The remodelling plan

The aim of the proposals was to reduce the workload of teachers, allowing them to do higher level planning, assessment and teaching, and so raise pupil achievement. When implemented the proposals will redefine the roles, responsibilities and relationships between teachers and a range of support staff in school. Also, the number of support staff will be increased and a wider range of such staff introduced, including senior assistants who could undertake some teaching activities (higher level teaching assistants). It is proposed that more adults with appropriate skills and experience carry out many of the organizational and administrative tasks currently performed by teachers, and contribute to pupils' learning through a more effective team approach. The government's remodelling plan has seven parts:

1 Changes to teachers' contracts to ensure:

(a) teachers not to be routinely required to undertake a range of administrative tasks (see the list of 24 tasks in Table 2.1), with effect from September 2003

(b) provision must be made for teachers and headteachers to enjoy a reasonable work-life balance, with effect from September 2003

(c) teachers not to be required to cover for absent colleagues for more than 38 hours within their 1,265 hours, with effect from September 2004

(d) teachers to get guaranteed time for planning, preparation and assessment (PPA), with effect from September 2005

(e) headteachers and senior managers to be guaranteed time for leadership duties by September 2005.

Table 2.1	Tasks that teachers should not have to do (DfES, 2002)	
Collecting money	Processing exam results	Stocktaking
Chasing absences	Collating pupil reports	Cataloguing, preparing
Bulk photocopying	Administering work experience	Issuing and maintaining equipment and materials
Copy typing	Administering examinations	Minuting meetings
Producing standard letters	Invigilating examinations	Co-ordinating and submitting bids
Producing class lists	Administering teacher cover	Seeking and giving personnel advice
Record-keeping and filing	ICT troubleshooting and minor repairs	Managing pupil data and inputting pupil data
Classroom display	Commissioning new ICT equipment	Ordering supplies and equipment
Analysing attendance figures		

In addition the government wishes to see a reduction in the extreme hours worked by some teachers and a reduction in the average term-time working week of 52 hours, but this should not be written into the teachers' contract.

2 A concerted attack on unnecessary paperwork and bureaucratic processes for teachers and heads, with an Implementation Review Unit with representation from headteachers and others, from September 2003.

3 Help for schools to achieve progressive reductions in teachers' hours over the next four years.

4 Additional school support staff to be recruited to act as 'personal assistants' to teachers.

5 New types of school support staff to take on more demanding roles in the classroom, for which appropriate training will be developed and provided but with their work supervised by a person with Qualified Teacher Status (QTS).

6 New managers and others with experience from outside education to be recruited to contribute to school management teams.

7 Headteachers to be supported by a national 'change management' programme, to help achieve in their schools the necessary reforms of the teaching profession and restructuring of the school workforce (adapted from TEN PB38, 2002).

This is how it looks when it's mapped out over the years:

September 2003

- 24 administrative tasks no longer to be done by teachers.

- Schools to consider teachers' work-life balance.

- Leadership and management time introduced for teachers with management responsibilities.

September 2004

- A 38-hour annual limit on covering for absent teachers.

September 2005

- Guaranteed time – 10 per cent of normal timetabled teaching time – for lesson planning and preparation.

- Teachers no longer invigilate exams.

- Dedicated leadership time for heads.

Some schools are implementing things earlier than strictly necessary. One can see the reasoning behind having a staggered approach but it makes things difficult. For instance, someone posted this comment on the *Times Educational Supplement* website in March 2004:

We appointed a 'teachers' secretary' to work X hours per week. She complains of not having enough work. Why? Because to fill her time teachers have to plan ahead – but due to PPA not coming on stream till 2005 in primary schools many of us still end up planning day to day or using our Sundays. Ergo, we do the work and our paid support twiddles her thumbs. We will only be able to use our support more effectively when we have time to plan for its use.

Transforming School Workforce Pathfinder Project

Many of the ideas about remodelling have come from the Transforming School Workforce Pathfinder Project that was launched in January 2002. The 32 pathfinder schools explored new ways to use their workforce and resources so that teachers can spend more time teaching, thus raising standards. The Department for Education and Skills (DfES) funded project had £4 million to spend. Schools and teachers were to find out what works best for them and share that knowledge with other schools around the country. The project aimed to secure significant reductions in the weekly hours worked by teachers and to increase the proportion of the week that is spent teaching. These aims were secured through:

- providing schools with consultancy support (school workforce advisers)
- training headteachers in change management
- allocating additional funds for employing additional teaching assistants
- providing information and communications technology (ICT) hardware and software
- funding the bursarial training of school managers.

In addition, funds were available for capital build such as additional office space for new management/administration staff.

Given these resources, the teachers made a number of suggestions and strategies:

1. Time: teachers asked for more time to do their work within the day. Primary school teachers wanted to be given non-contact time, and secondary teachers wanted to have their non-contact time protected. Teachers wanted time to do planning, marking, and to do lesson observations.

2. Teachers: there was a call from some teachers for more teachers, but also there was a need for the roles and responsibilities of teachers to be clarified. Teachers wanted to be trusted to know their job and to be able to exercise their professional judgement.

3. Smaller classes: there was a call from some teachers for smaller classes in order to reduce marking and pupil behaviour difficulties.

4. Reduce bureaucracy: teachers argued that there was a need for a more simplified approach to assessment. The generation and management of data could be better organised. In particular, ICT could be used better to store, prevent replication and enable easier access to data.

5. Government initiatives: there was the view that the number of initiatives should be reduced, and that schools should be given more flexibility to develop their own plans.

6 Support staff: teachers were asking for more and better use of support staff. In particular, they identified the need for clerical and administrative support for teaching, and for curriculum areas/subject departments/faculties.

7 Teaching assistants: there was a demand for more, better deployed, better trained teaching assistants. There was a need for planning time for teachers and teaching assistants (adapted from Thomas et al., 2003).

WHAT HELP IS THERE?

In the first year of the roll-out, 2003, 1,000 schools were involved in the remodelling process, with a further 7,500 planned by mid-2005. By 2006 every school in England (some 23,500) will be taking part in the remodelling programme. There are 'early adopter' schools in every LEA, but they do not receive extra funding. However, there are lots of support systems, as shown in Figure 2.1. The national organizations include the DfES and the General Teaching Council (GTC) but also:

● the Workforce Agreement Monitoring Group (WAMG) – made up of representatives of the Signatories to the National Agreement, which publishes regular notes of guidance such as:

  – WAMG Note 8 (15 March 2004) – identifying a number of emerging 'success factors' that characterize those LEAs that are leading the way in implementing the reforms

  – WAMG Note 6 (15 December 2003) – guidance for schools to consider when deploying staff to carry out cover supervision

● the Teacher Training Agency (TTA) – responsible for training and assessing higher level teaching assistants

Figure 2.1	The support network for remodelling

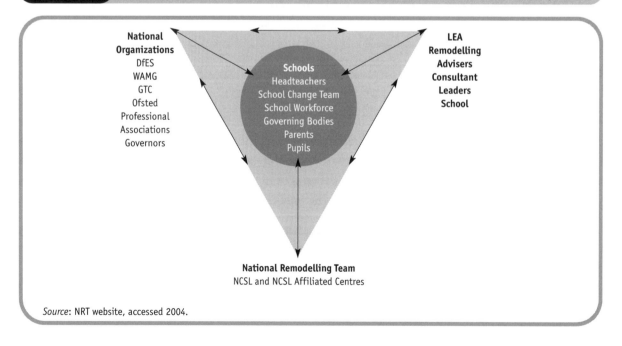

Source: NRT website, accessed 2004.

- Ofsted – responsible for monitoring whether schools have implemented the remodelling agenda

- professional associations – except for the National Union of Teachers, which did not sign the workload agreement.

The National Remodelling Team (NRT) was set up in 2002 by the DfES to provide resources and advice to help implement the national agreement. It has taken suggestions from the Pathfinder Project forward; seeing remodelling as having the potential to enhance the status and work-life balance of all who work in the education sector and to improve pupils' learning opportunities and standards of achievement. The model of change they propose is outlined in Chapter 3.

Remodelling consultants work with LEAs to support and advise individual schools as they work through their change management process. They help the LEA remodelling adviser and others who may be used by the LEA to support the rollout. The National College for School Leadership (NCSL – and its regional affiliated centres) is also supporting remodelling. Consultant leaders give extra help to specific schools. Each school sets up a school change team; and we explain more about this in the next chapter.

One of the key places to find out information is the website run by the National Remodelling Team. This offers news and advice on all the latest developments in remodelling. It includes a comprehensive 'explainer', documenting what remodelling is, an ideas bank to point you towards solutions to your problems and a case study section. For person-to-person advice, classroom teachers and assistants can ask their senior manager or union representative; senior managers can go to their LEA remodelling advisers, who in turn can seek advice from ten regional advisers. The whole industry is geared towards making the provisions of the agreement a reality. The appendix and reference sections at the end of this book contain the addresses of many useful websites and publications.

Cutting bureaucracy

A significant cause of excessive workload in schools has been the growth of paperwork. The workforce agreement resulted in the setting up in April 2003 of the Implementation Review Unit (IRU). This independent body, made up largely of practising heads, aims to help schools cut 'red tape' and reduce bureaucracy. From its discussions and visits to schools, the Unit notes that the most commonly identified bureaucracy concerns were:

- multiple bidding for separate funding streams

- initiative overload

- the special educational needs system

- overzealous monitoring and evaluation of schools

- duplicated requests from outside organizations, and overlapping roles of education agencies

- administering exams/tests

- recruiting and retaining staff (IRU, 2003).

Schools welcomed the establishment of a panel of serving practitioners advising DfES Ministers and when asked which achievements would be needed to consider the IRU a success, many comments were received many of which related to workload and unnecessary paperwork. The IRU has already identified some of the things that LEAs are doing to reduce bureaucracy and information overload, such as:

- consultation arrangements with a (small) group of headteachers to gather views on whether 'questionable' information/data requests, etc. should be forwarded to all schools

- random checks at individual schools to view the contents of the school's post bag and obtain a 'picture' of the mail schools are receiving

- a termly index of the previous term's mailings; identifying for schools at the end of term the likely mailings that are likely to be sent to schools during the next term

- providing schools with a number of email addresses, which can be individually targeted to different members of staff

- dedicated pages on schools' inter/intranet sites designed for different members of school staff

- a 'traffic light' system identifying the importance of items appearing on the schools' inter/intranet

- restricting 'all schools' email addresses to a limited number of officers and letters to 'All Headteachers' personally agreed/signed by the Director

- consideration of at what point it becomes more economic to distribute a document in paper form rather than electronically (with the expectation that schools will have to print off the document)

- communications (electronic/paper) to schools provided with a short cover sheet explaining the content of the communication and for whom intended

- development of a central LEA 'warehouse' of school data coupled with a requirement that data requests are first submitted to the 'warehouse' – before being made of schools – where the data may already exist (IRU, 2003).

Cover

Cover supervision by effectively deployed support staff with appropriate skills and training is a fundamental part of an effective cover strategy, increasing the options available to headteachers and allowing them to deal with teacher absence in a way which is compatible with the standards agenda and the efficient use of resources.

Thus, an important part of the workforce reforms has been the introduction of a new level of support staff, people with higher level teaching assistant (HLTA) status. Some schools have already been using teaching assistants as 'cover supervisors' but these HLTAs will be able to cover or supervise classes, while teachers are planning, preparing, undergoing professional development or are absent. The first 300 were assessed in Spring 2004 and there is to be a national roll-out of training and assessment from September 2004. Teaching assistants have to meet the specifically designed HLTA Standards (TTA, 2003). We discuss these and other issues at greater depth in Chapter 7.

STAFF WELLBEING

Many things are happening under the general heading of staff wellbeing including a number of 'stress-busting' and work-life balance initiatives, but the most important developments are probably the Healthy Schools initiative and the Well-Being Programme. An increasing number of schools are involved in these two related government initiatives.

In 1999 the Department for Education and Employment (as it was then) and the Department of Health jointly published the National Healthy School Standard (NHSS) which provided guidelines on how to access local healthy schools programmes. It was part of the government's drive to reduce health inequalities, promote social inclusion and raise educational standards (Healthy Schools initiative website). It provides a framework within which local healthy schools programmes can tackle inequalities and aims to improve the health and emotional wellbeing of young people and adults. It was introduced in October 1999 as a vehicle to support delivery of personal, social and health education (PSHE) and citizenship in schools. This message was reinforced in November 1999 when the Qualifications and Curriculum Authority (QCA) published the national PSHE/Citizenship Framework, which emphasized the whole school approach advocated in the standard.

The NHSS is designed to give as much practical support as possible for schools to create an enjoyable, safe, productive learning environment and to minimize potential health risks. The 2002 publication *Staff Health and Wellbeing* (Health Development Agency, DH/DfES, 2002), demonstrates convincingly why promoting staff health and wellbeing is key to developing a 'healthy school'. In addition it outlines some important principles and how they might inform practice, and provides examples of how staff health and wellbeing approaches are being implemented in different parts of the country. For any school considering staff health and wellbeing this is an excellent introduction (the publication is available from the Health Development Agency or from the above website) and, although written mainly for local healthy schools programme co-ordinators, it merits careful reading by school leaders.

Worklife Support was set up in 1999 by the international charity for teachers, Teacher Support Network. Its work can be divided into three related areas:

1   Employee Assistance Programmes.

2   Well-Being Programme.

3   Training and development (tailored to the school's needs and usually linked to the aforementioned programmes).

Worklife Support offers schools independent and confidential advice, support and counselling to staff (at all levels) on a wide range of work-related and personal issues. For example, this may involve managing workload, relationships with colleagues, pupils and parents, dealing with stress, achieving a better work-life balance, financial and debt counselling, personal counselling, or support on family matters and legal advice.

Health and wellbeing initiatives in a school are said to benefit the whole school community, through the realization that a school is not only an educational establishment but also a workplace. For instance, one of the health issues identified by the Newbattle Cluster Health Promoting School Working Group in Midlothian, Scotland, was staff health/stress. A small working group was set up with its main aim being to alleviate staff stress. The three areas tackled were:

- To raise awareness of stress in the workplace. This was done by signposting relevant inservice education and training opportunities for staff, i.e. recognizing stress indicators.

- To provide stress-alleviating initiatives. A programme of short-term activities was developed to support health including massage, pilates, swimming and yoga.

- Improvement to workplace environment, to make it more conducive to good health. The staff facilities, toilets, wash facilities, display boards and indoor plants were upgraded.

Well-Being Programme

The Well-Being Programme, is also run by Worklife Support, but was set up by the Teacher Support Network, again in 1999. It began (in conjunction with the National Healthy Schools initiative) as a pilot project in Norfolk but has rapidly expanded and now involves about 800 schools in 40 LEAs and has recently expanded to over 400 schools in London. In some cases, LEAs finance the programme; in others, individual schools contract Worklife Support (it can cost up to £1,900 for a large secondary school); and in London the DfES is subsidizing some schools.

The Well-Being Programme is well designed and involves a series of stages, as shown in Figure 2.2. Once a school has signed up, the school appoints one or two facilitators from amongst the staff (stage 2 in Figure 2.2). Their role is to promote good practice, good communication and a positive approach to problem-solving. They will give wellbeing a high profile within their school and help colleagues to find the most appropriate sources of help when they need it. In many cases, schools are nominating one member of the teaching staff and one member of the support staff to ensure that representation is as broad as possible. The facilitators receive a day of preparation (stage 3), which includes providing resources and setting up networks.

Figure 2.2	The structure of the Well-Being Project

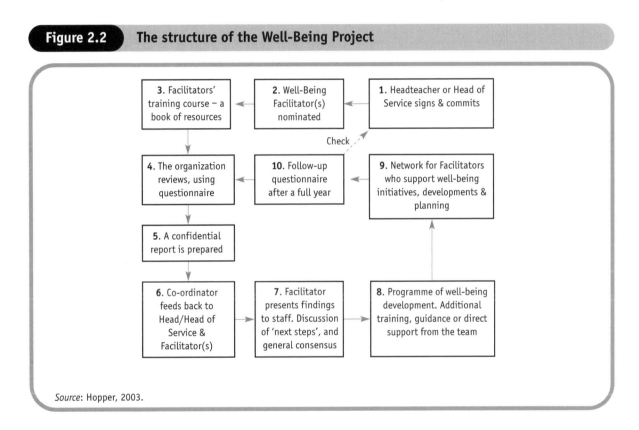

Source: Hopper, 2003.

Stage 4 is the organizational self-review (OSR) which is an on-line questionnaire based on the seven areas of wellbeing identified by the Health and Safety Executive (*culture; demands; control; relationships; change; role; support, training and individual factors*). Staff have to say how much they agree or disagree with a series of statements such as:

- The organization meets the individual's professional development needs.

- People are being fairly treated.

- Everybody will pull together in times of stress, or when the going gets tough.

- There is good, open communication between staff and managers.

- I feel my contribution is valued.

- In times of change we feel part of the process.

- We can and do achieve a good work/life balance.

- I rarely think my job is dull or boring.

Schools have found a number of ways of ensuring that all staff can complete the questionnaire, including:

- setting up a computer suite for staff to access during and after the school day

- facilitators helping staff who are less confident about using a computer

- paying support staff for an additional half hour

- timing the organizational self-review to coincide with an INSET or training day

- closing the school half an hour early to enable staff to complete the organizational self-review (Hopper, 2003)

In order to protect anonymity, data are only available for groups of at least ten (stage 5). Small schools may only generate one set of graphs for the entire staff group. Larger schools, however, may have access to data on separate demographic groups, such as teachers and support staff and full-time and part-time staff. The data are used by the LEA Well-Being Co-ordinator to prepare a detailed confidential report, which is then discussed with senior management and the facilitator(s) (stage 6), and the main areas for development are identified. The facilitator presents the findings of the benchmark review to a meeting of the staff (stage 7).

Lancashire LEA was able to see the big picture from data from all the schools that completed the OSR. Brenda Hopper, the LEA co-ordinator, found that:

- The highest scoring section was 'relationships'. This is probably not surprising, as the schools that joined the programme tended to be those where staff wellbeing is seen as important, where the senior management recognizes the value of their staff, and of investing in them.

- Workloads and pressures were areas of common concern. These were particularly high for teaching staff, placing a real strain on home and family lives. There was also evidence that many support staff, particularly those working full time in classrooms, were experiencing greater pressure and feeling more stressed than they had previously.

- Most people considered that 'improving the physical environment' and 'acknowledging our achievements' were priorities.

- Support staff wanted more career development opportunities (Hopper, 2003, p. 47).

Carol Lynch, director of Worklife Support says that these are common themes in most schools:

When you look at the national data, you see that people who work in schools are proud of their achievements and don't always feel that that is celebrated enough. People who work in schools believe in their jobs and that they are making a real contribution. There is peer support for staff, but there isn't always a good link with management. The management of change is a big issue; people want to feel involved in the process of change. Looking at work/life balance and workload continues to be an issue, as is communication.

(TSN website)

A programme is developed that is tailored to the needs of the school (stage 8). The programme may include an element of additional training, guidance or direct support from the co-ordinator and/or from external consultants (stage 9). A follow-up questionnaire is completed by staff a year later (stage 10), which is used to identify changes and highlight next steps for the school.

Hopper (2003) notes that evidence is beginning to emerge that in some schools, despite the high levels of pressure and heavy workloads, staff feel engaged, cared for and included, and able to cope with the pressures. She claims that they even manage to achieve a reasonably good work-life balance.

The Teacher Support Network commissioned a small piece of research in Norfolk where the scheme was first piloted with around 100 schools between 1999 and 2002. The main findings, which are based on the questionnaire returns of 84 primary, middle, secondary and special school heads, are given in Figure 2.3. Most schools at the time of the survey (November 2003) had been involved in the programme for at least a year.

Figure 2.3   **The effects of the Well-Being project on 84 Norfolk schools**

Overall school impact
- 89% of headteachers rated school culture and ethos better or much better
- 86% of headteachers rated overall school effectiveness better or much better
- 85% of headteachers rated overall school community better or much better
- 68% of headteachers rated the physical work environment better or much better

Recruitment and retention
- 57% of headteachers rated recruitment of new staff better or much better
- 67% of headteachers rated retention of new staff better or much better
- 70% of headteachers rated retention of existing staff better or much better
- 62% of headteachers rated improvements in staff absenteeism and supply costs as better or much better
- 65% of headteachers felt telling potential new recruits about Well-Being project increased the likelihood of them accepting the job

Effects on pupils
- 85% of headteachers rated pupil behaviour and morale better or much better
- 73% of headteachers rated pupil results and performance better or much better
- 93% of headteachers rated communication between staff and pupils better or much better

Staff performance, communication and morale
- 88% of headteachers rated staff performance better or much better
- 80% of headteachers rated communication between staff better or much better
- 80% of headteachers rated morale better or much better

Source: TSN website.

RECRUITMENT AND RETENTION

The final area we wish to consider concerns the recruitment and retention of staff, especially teachers. We have already noted how recruitment and retention have been important factors when considering workload, remodelling and wellbeing, clearly they go together. Schools will be able to add to their recruitment incentives by pointing to the benefits of remodelling, for example by being a cover-free school, where marking and preparation time is already more than 10 per cent and where a policy on work-life balance has led to reducing the hours people are expected to work.

Similarly, schools that have achieved 'Investors in People' or which are 'Healthy Schools' will have an edge on those who are not. We saw for example how in Lancashire LEA a recruitment and retention strategy was part of the LEA's Education Development Plan and included opportunities for continuing professional development, whilst the Well-Being Programme was also part of the overall recruitment and retention strategy. Nearly all LEAs have appointed recruitment strategy managers and are working closely with schools and offering advice (Ofsted, 2002). Recruitment strategies used by LEAs include improving the quality of information to NQTs; supporting the employment based route to qualified teacher status; the graduate training programme (GTP); maintaining a supply teacher register; running return to teaching courses; recruiting from overseas; and supporting school governors.

Ofsted found that LEA strategies concerning retention were less firmly established but they were beginning to recognize the need to offer an attractive career package for school staff. For example, one LEA surveys teachers within their first year of teaching to find out what further training and development are required, as well as offering sustained CPD to build the leadership potential of young staff. Others offer high-quality induction programmes and make use of salary, housing, transport and relocation incentives. Exit questionnaires were also being used more to establish reasons for leaving with a view to addressing any factors that may arise preventing the school or LEA from being a 'good employer'.

Paying greater attention to staff welfare, addressing wellbeing and valuing what they do is all part of being a 'good employer' and such employers have less difficulty in employing staff and retaining them. Chapter 8 has more ideas about good management practice that will help recruit and retain staff.

IN CONCLUSION: IN PRACTICE

The remodelling website has many case studies and diaries of schools that are going through the restructuring process and redesigning the workforce. They paint a very positive picture and have many ideas and lessons for others to learn from. However, the process is not without its difficulties and these postings from the *Times Educational Supplement* website's virtual staff room give an alternative view of what things were like in Spring 2004 in transferring the 24 tasks:

> *Our school doesn't seem to have changed much since the workload agreement. My TA [teaching assistant] put up one display and my mentor came in and 'had a word' about letting my assistant do all the work!!!*

> *It really isn't that easy as an NQT to stand up in a new school and loudly proclaim you are refusing to do something when we all know that everybody, (including SMT) is simply trying their damnedest to just keep heads above the water!*

> *The workload agreement sounds wonderful in practice and my new department has been provided with a lovely clerical assistant who has no place to sit in the whole school, and who cannot possible be expected to do the photocopying of a 15 strong department nor put up those teachers' displays.*

> *At our school there is a meeting that everyone must attend about reducing workload. So, they turn up to the meeting (after school no doubt until about 5pm) when everyone goes home and then stays up late doing the work they couldn't do earlier because of the meeting. If you want to reduce workload it is easy! I could do it! You simply say about a particular initiative – we are no longer doing it. Simple. SAT mocks – forget it. Interim reports – stopped. Performance Management – furnace time. In fact, very few people who talk about reducing workload are actually committed to it because whenever it gets mentioned life seems to get more not less stressful.*

> (postings on the TES website's virtual staff room, March 2004)

These are fair points! The key to the success of initiatives to do with remodelling, wellbeing and workload is to integrate them into what schools are already doing, so that they are not seen as 'add-ons'. As Hopper notes: 'the priorities that the school identifies for action need to be part of the school development plan, complementing other activities within the school and making clear and explicit links to other programmes and developments' (2003, p. 43). There are no easy answers, but the following chapters attempt to unpack the issues further. The next chapter deals with the crucial area of the management of change.

Section B

How do you change it?

Chapter 3

Why is managing change not easy?

- What is change and why change?
- Why managing change is complex
- Models for changing workload and wellbeing
- Lessons to be learned

The focus of this chapter is change management. How do we ensure change is managed successfully to ensure everyone's wellbeing and that stress is minimized? What do we know about successful change that we need to consider when leading and managing the change process? And what about remodelling, workload and wellbeing – what sorts of changes are being introduced as a result of these initiatives and what models of the change process underpin them? Stoll et al. (2003) assert that to succeed in a world characterized by rapid change and increased complexity, it is vital that schools grow, develop, adapt creatively to and take charge of change so that they can create their own preferable future. In this chapter we consider what makes for success and why things may not always work out as planned. It is hoped that by the end of this chapter you will have a better understanding of all these questions and, perhaps more importantly, some possible answers as well! Understanding the nature of change and how we react to it can help us manage and lead it more effectively.

WHAT IS CHANGE AND WHY CHANGE?

Schools and colleges are continually changing. You don't need us to tell you that recent educational changes have been extensive and affected all areas of school life and age groups. They have come from different sources and can be considered in three main categories: change required or encouraged by central government policy and legislation, change resulting from external inspections, and changes initiated by schools themselves, sometimes from the head and senior team (top down) and sometimes from teachers and other staff (bottom up).

Change is by definition a natural part of life. Morrison (1998) in one of the most comprehensive discussions of change and its management currently available, defines change as:

> *A dynamic and continuous process of development and growth that involves a reorganisation in response to 'felt needs'. It is a process of transformation, a flow from one state to another, either initiated by internal factors or external forces, involving individuals, groups or institutions, leading to a realignment of existing values, practices and outcomes.*

Morrison's main conclusion is that change concerns people more than content and that 'successful management is about managing successful change'. This means managing people successfully.

As we noted in Chapter 1, one of the main findings of the PriceWaterhouseCoopers report (2001) was that teachers in many schools perceived a lack of control and ownership over their work and, although many welcomed the spirit of many government initiatives, they felt that: 'the pace and manner of change was working against achieving high standards, that they were insufficiently supported to meet these changes, and not accorded the professional trust that they merited' (p. 1). Both heads and teachers felt unsupported and that the speed and manner of implementation of change had added significantly to their workload. According to PwC, what was needed was a reduction in teacher workload, an increase in teacher ownership and, most importantly, the capacity created for managing change in a sustainable way that would prepare the ground for school improvement. At the heart of the National Remodelling Programme is 'a fundamental belief that deep-seated change can and does occur – what it requires are new attitudes and behaviours, new beliefs and values, and new skills and capabilities to be created and, importantly, sustained' (see NRT website).

WHY MANAGING CHANGE IS COMPLEX

Managing change is a difficult and complex task for a number of reasons. Much organizational change is unplanned and unpredictable. Planned change needs to be balanced with continuity to maintain personal and organizational equilibrium. Most of the work of school managers is concerned with maintaining routine day-to-day activities, principally the teaching and learning programmes. Too much change leads to 'initiative fatigue' and 'innovation overload'; too little leads to stagnation.

It is often assumed that planned change will be beneficial for those involved. Innovation, however, in altering existing arrangements, is both personally and organizationally threatening and brings losses as well as gains. Any change, however small, is likely to disadvantage one or more of those concerned.

We tend to look for instant results from change, but it may take many years before the results of large-scale change can be properly assessed, particularly where student outcomes are concerned. Our 'maps of change are faulty' (Fullan, 1993); they portray innovation as a simple, rational journey following a logical path from policy-making to implementation. However, we can identify at least four main stages in the management of the change process. These are initiation, implementation, continuation or institutionalization, and outcomes. The process, however, is not a simple linear progression: it's a two-way process and events at any stage may feed back to alter decisions made at a previous stage. Thus, in implementing a particular change there may prove to be unintended and unexpected consequences in practice, which lead us back to reconsider the original purposes of the innovation determined at the initiation stage. Similarly, the original purposes and plans for the innovation are interpreted and adapted by those putting it into practice, so the final outcomes may be very different from what was originally intended. Change is thus a long-term process not a simple event. Many changes fail to progress beyond the planning or early implementation stage.

Those managing change have to deal with multiple changes, each progressing through the various stages noted above. The changes interact and impact on each other and may not be mutually compatible.

Factors affecting change are many but a simple yet very helpful model has been put forward by Martin and Holt (2002) in a book for school governors. They see successful change as part of a 'change equation' made up of five components, all of which are required to be present. The omission of any one can lead to problems (see Figure 3.1). For instance, if there are vision, skills, incentives and resources but no action plans the result will be false starts.

Figure 3.1   The change equation

Vision	Skills	Incentives	Resources	Action Plans	= Change
******	Skills	Incentives	Resources	Action Plans	= Confusion
Vision	******	Incentives	Resources	Action Plans	= Anxiety
Vision	Skills	******	Resources	Action Plans	= Gradual change
Vision	Skills	Incentives	******	Action Plans	= Frustration
Vision	Skills	Incentives	Resources	******	= False starts

Source: Martin and Holt, 2002, p. 37

Changes affecting schools may be initiated at any of the decision-making levels in the education system:

- central/national (e.g. DfES, funding bodies)

- local education authority

- school (i.e. head/senior management team)

- department or subunit

- individual teacher.

Decision-makers at different levels within the system have differing ideologies and change agendas, based on differing perspectives on the goals of education and the means of bringing these about. Even within the school there are multiple goals. Wherever the change originated, it has to be managed through the various stages shown above, at the three levels within the organization. There may be an 'implementation gap' between the intentions of policy-makers at national level and what is actually implemented in schools and classrooms. Similarly, you may be able to identify an 'implementation gap' in the management of change between different levels in your own school. The process is further complicated when implementation problems at one level require a review of decisions made at another level (see Open University, 1997, pp. 73–4).

At its simplest, managing change means recognizing the 4 Ps: purpose, picture, plan and part. The basic purpose for the change has to be clear and people need to understand why the change is needed. A picture needs to be painted of the outcomes of the change and this is part of the vision-building process. We need to encourage ownership of the change or 'buy in' as the Americans call it. It is also necessary to produce and discuss an outline plan which should be included in the school's development or improvement plan. It will need to be modified during implementation. Finally, each person should be given a part to play in both the plan and the outcome itself – they need to know how they can contribute and participate.

Fullan (2001) talks about a number of concrete factors to keep in mind when considering change, for example, the use of resistance to good effect (redefining resistance so it's seen in a positive and not negative light); the expectation of dips in the process; the requirement for reculturing; the need for pressure and support; that change takes time; and people need to understand the innovation and what it is trying to achieve. He puts complexity together with moral purpose and collaboration towards a common goal as his formula for successful change. As he noted in an earlier work: 'The crux of change is how individuals understand and experience the proposed change' (Fullan, 1991). Those implementing change can often forget how others will feel as a result of it.

Ofsted has recently noted that schools that manage their workforce effectively do a number of things (see Chapter 8), including managing change by harnessing the energies of staff to plan for and introduce changes that lead to better teaching and higher standards (Ofsted, 2004). They do this by seeing the potential benefits to the school of changes, including those initiated by government, and present them to staff in a positive light, taking care to stage and time their introduction. These changes, Ofsted suggest, have generally had a positive effect on the deployment, motivation, development and performance of teachers.

Secondly, Ofsted found that information and communication technology (ICT) was used increasingly to support effective management and teaching, and funding was used well to improve ICT resources and develop the skills of staff in their use. Finally, Ofsted note how school managers monitored the effect of their decisions on the work of the school through self-evaluation and external review, and took account of the findings in future planning (Ofsted, 2004).

Managing resistance and conflict

Resistance is a natural response to feelings of 'loss, anxiety and struggle' (Busher and Harris, 2000, p. 19). Change for many is synonymous with extra work, pressure and stress. Resistance should therefore be anticipated as a natural part of the change process. Westhuizen (as quoted by Blandford, 1999) sums it up neatly:

When change is implemented in the school, a disturbance of the status quo occurs. The school as an organisation and more specifically, the teachers in the school react to the change by generating energy (resistance) to maintain the internal or existing equilibrium of the status quo. The energy that is generated at either the acceptance, but mostly at the rejection, upsets the balance. The result of the complex factors that give rise to this is usually perceived as resistance to change.

(p. 180)

According to Busher and Harris (2000, p. 20), 'A major reason for the failure of change at both school and subject area level lies in a lack of attention to the process of change'. It is very important to think through the change process carefully in order to reduce the number of negative side effects. Remember too, as noted above, resistance can be used to good effect, it gets you to think through your ideas and to ask yourself 'are we on the right track?'

Sergiovanni (1994) reminds us that schools are made up of individuals, all of whom have their own particular agendas. Therefore, it is the job of school leaders to combine agendas to the common aims of the school. School leaders influence teams to work collaboratively together, to share vision, to motivate and to perform. School leaders must try to empower staff by making public their own professional educational values and sharing them. This way, an agreed collegiate culture can be created, encouraging a learning environment for all staff and pupils

(Earley and Bubb, 2004; Gold et al., 2003). Commitment and collegiality in others has to be developed, and school leaders need to involve staff in decision-making, allowing them to take ownership of their work, valuing them, and translating clear vision and purpose. The development of a collegiate culture or a culture of collaboration, consultation and shared decision-making is the most important factor for successful change. Remember that the process is as important as the change itself.

Strategies to help overcome resistance to change can include ensuring people are given sufficient information about the change and its desired effect; greater involvement in the design and implementation of the change; negotiating with staff if they feel they are going to lose out; and being supportive, listening to any doubts and concerns people may have and providing training as needed.

Training and development plays a key role in the change process – and not only at the implementation stage. When trying to implement change, anxiety and worry will be reduced if additional training is provided through various mediums such as peer mentoring, observations, shadowing, research, courses, etc. It is also essential, however, that effective professional development is focused on classroom change and on developing new techniques and teaching behaviours. Remember that any changes regarding workload and wellbeing should ultimately be about improving the pupils' learning experience (Redhead, 2004).

However, when intending to implement change one will almost certainly be confronted not only with resistance but also with some kind of conflict. The ability to handle conflict is a key factor in successful change management. Dealing with conflict can often create a sense of fear but it is important to remember that conflict, like resistance, is an inevitable part of implementing change and that one must therefore: 'understand its source, empathise with those overcome by it and have strategies to deal with it' (Gold and Evans, 1998, p. 42).

When managed effectively, conflict and resistance can be quite positive. As noted by Gold and Evans: 'well managed conflict can be productive and creative and can move a group of people or an organisation on to a far more productive phase than the one it was 'stuck' in before' (1998, p. 43). Managing conflict is often synonymous with managing difficult people. Mismanaging those members of our team who create problems for it can impede change but, more drastically, impede development for that individual. When dealing with difficult people, Gold and Evans (1998, p. 44) suggest that we should:

- acknowledge uncomfortable feelings aroused in you by different persons, put them aside and work objectively

- separate person from problem

- take time – do not react immediately. Think about your next action to make it proactive

- plan your actions carefully – rehearse what you are going to say.

It is also important to ensure that we do not allow ourselves to become manipulative or aggressive.

MODELS FOR CHANGING WORKLOAD AND WELLBEING

And what about remodelling, workload and wellbeing – what sorts of changes are being introduced as a result of these initiatives and what models of the change process underpin them? As the National Remodelling Team (NRT) note on their website, 'remodelling involves change. Understanding and managing change is a key part of the school remodelling process and one which can often prove the most difficult'. Interestingly, the evaluators of the Transforming School Workforce Pathfinder Project note that the process of change was itself seen as a valuable outcome, creating a mood shift towards change (Thomas et al., 2004). Changes in the 32 pathfinder schools included:

- remodelling staff roles and responsibilities

- staff reviewing their work and workload

- restructuring the school day and week

- using ICT to support learning, such as the use of electronic whiteboards.

The evaluation team remark how some of these changes highlight an issue related to the boundaries between the Pathfinder Project and other initiatives in which schools were involved. They note that: 'In some of the schools, successful implementation seems associated with schools having created almost seamless links between projects. Indeed, securing change in schools might seem to be more likely if new initiatives are introduced into a school in a way that demonstrates linkage and integration with existing activities' (Thomas et al., 2004, p. 10).

Amongst the pathfinder schools the change process has been approached in slightly different ways:

1 At Manor Hall Middle school in West Sussex volunteers were recruited for a School Change Team. The team comprised representatives from across the school including a NQT, a teacher, the head, the deputy head, an office staff member, a midday supervisor, a cleaner, a governor and a parent.

2 At Beacon Hall School the approach was to develop distributed leadership through an inclusive approach to participation in, and responsibility for, change. All staff are members of one of six change teams and each team

worked on a particular change goal e.g. homework, ICT and the curriculum. Staff were encouraged to engage in 'blue skies thinking' and to have open debates which generated strategies that were taken forward.

3　Pembury Primary school already had a strategic team, comprising of the headteacher, the deputy, the special educational needs coordinator (SENCO) and Key Stage 1 (KS1) and Key Stage 2 (KS2) representatives but this was disbanded as one of the first stages of the remodelling process. Catherine Thewlis the headteacher says 'It wasn't a good way of really implementing bottom-up change'. The change team includes representatives from throughout the school. Each member of the old strategic team recruited another member of staff, and there are representatives of support staff, governor and parents. There are also more negative staff in the change team. 'We need to understand why they are negative' she explains. 'It'll help them to see the big picture, and being involved in the change process may well change their attitudes.' The head attended the first meeting of the change team, but stayed out of further meetings. She believes she could be an inhibitor on them really expressing their dissatisfactions and coming up with truly innovative ideas.

Sustainability is a key factor in change and whether the additional resources, often seen as critical in enabling the changes to take place, would be sustained. However, 'set against these concerns was the recognition in some of the schools that the Project had given them confidence to begin to manage resources more creatively, creating a newfound sense of freedom' (Thomas et al., 2004, p. 11).

National Remodelling Team approach

Building on the work of the Pathfinder Project, the National Remodelling Team has developed its own approach to change management, which it is deploying with the 'early adopter' schools in 150 LEAs – the successors to the Pathfinders but without the extra resources! The approach to change management is said to be most successful when five key elements are addressed:

1　The school change team contains representatives from all staff levels within the school.

2　Political, emotional and practical factors are considered for each prospective change.

3　There is a willingness to collaborate, both within the school and with other schools and bodies outside the school.

4　School representatives attend regional remodelling events.

5　An external mentor, usually a remodelling consultant, is engaged as a 'critical friend', to give an outside perspective and additional insight on the changes proposed.

A key question for schools is: 'Are there opportunities for improvement and do we need to be asking some hard questions?' A school must first identify the need and desire for change – mobilisation – before moving on to the four stages of the change process – the 4 Ds:

1   *Discover*. Participants realize that the school is doing many good things already, but certain aspects need to be improved. The main aims are to uncover the issues around workload, assess the readiness for change and start to build commitment.

2   *Deepen*. A number of problem-solving techniques are used so that participants can fully understand the scale and scope of the change required. There may be no obvious route to a solution, but everybody's clear that something's got to change. It's crucial to recognize the emotional and political barriers to change before being able to move on.

3   *Develop*. Using problem-solving and teambuilding techniques the school change team (SCT) begin to develop possible solutions. It's up to the SCT to define a clear vision of the future and to define the change programme they need to achieve that vision. There's no magic formula – every approach needs to be tailored to the individual school. One size doesn't fit all.

4   *Deliver*. This stage develops the plan further and the vision of the future is shared with the whole school. Then it's all systems go as initial actions are started. A key factor at this stage is the establishment of a change culture within the school where staff have the confidence and excitement to maintain continuous improvement into the future.

The NRT has developed, trained and co-ordinated advisers and LEA facilitators who are helping schools understand the change process and supporting them in developing their own solutions, and learning from other schools.

More recently, a staff management and deployment self-evaluation checklist has been developed (see NRT website) for the NRT which includes the six-step review process outlined in Figure 3.2.

Figure 3.2   A six-step review process

- Step 1 – decide on the objectives of the review, e.g. for:
    the senior management team considering a staff restructuring
    the governors and senior management team developing new staffing policies
- Step 2 – determine the focus of the review.
- Step 3 – establish what evidence you need to meet your objective 1 at Step 1. Plan how to obtain this evidence. A key issue is to decide whom to involve in the process of answering the checklist questions.
- Step 4 – consider all the questions in the area(s) you are focusing on carefully. Answer them in light of your current knowledge and evidence.
- Step 5 – ask the questions and where necessary, probe to ensure responses are sound and balanced.
- Step 6 – implement agreed actions having regard to the objective(s), at Step 1, and monitor whether it has the intended impact on the school's performance.

Source: NRT 2003.

Well-Being Programme approach

We said in Chapter 2 that the Well-Being Programme was not meant to be seen as 'yet another initiative' but something that is integral to the school, and that the sponsors were committed to a bottom-up approach, creating a sense of ownership and responsibility within each individual and at every level. The change process underpinning the Well-Being Programme, is similar to that of others, commencing with a rigorous self-review which includes a questionnaire completed by each staff member. The change process comprises five steps:

Step 1: wellbeing facilitator(s) are established.

Step 2: staff in each participating school complete a benchmark review using a confidential on-line questionnaire and a detailed confidential report is prepared to be discussed with senior management and the facilitator(s), and the main areas for development are identified.

Step 3: the facilitator (with the support of the co-ordinator) presents the findings of the benchmark review to a meeting of the staff.

Step 4: a programme is developed that is tailored to the needs of the school. The programme may include an element of additional training, guidance or direct support from the co-ordinator and/or from external consultants.

Step 5: a follow-up questionnaire is completed by staff, which is used to identify changes and highlight next steps for the school (see Chapter 2 for further details).

LESSONS TO BE LEARNED

On the NRT website there are case studies of schools that have implemented change. We have drawn on advice and suggestions from Penryn High School, Kenton School, West Heath Junior School, the Thomas Lord Audley School and Language College, Manor Hall Middle School and Brunswick House Primary School for the lessons they have learned about the successful management of change as a result of trying to implement aspects of the remodelling agenda. These are shown in Figure 3.3.

Figure 3.3	Suggestions about managing change from case study schools

Do
- have a clear picture of where you want to go
- remember that if you waste teachers' time on things that don't really matter or that someone else could do, it's a waste of money, a waste of their training and professional experience and a waste of high-quality teaching and learning time as well.
- recognize that transferring work, as well as relieving teachers of tasks as well as responsibilities, creates both challenges and career opportunities for support staff
- remember that taking jobs away creates insecurity, just as any change brings uncertainty and takes time to work properly.
- ask everyone formally every year to share their good ideas on how to improve the efficiency of the school, on which jobs could be transferred to administrators rather than teachers and to make public those things which are working efficiently and those which create frustration and waste time and money
- articulate, celebrate and share the positive outcomes of the change process
- invest time to get everyone on board – consult and respond to all staff
- be bold and daring, have faith in your ideas, take calculated risks, think outside the box
- look at more effective ways of doing things
- seek value for money – make the budget work for you
- place the human requirements of the school community first
- recognize all the things you have done already
- take time to listen to all groups of staff (and pupils)
- provide encouragement and reassurance if someone feels anxious
- be patient because change takes time
- be willing to let go of existing work habits
- lead by example.

Don't
- reduce your teachers' workload in ways that would reduce the quality of your school's provision. Your pupils deserve the best.
- take on extra work yourself, in order to reduce your colleagues' workload.
- expect everything to happen instantly
- invest in ICT without adequate training and affordable technical back-up
- search for a 'quick fix'; think about long term growth and success
- walk past vested interests, have the courage to challenge the status quo
- think that moving a job to a non-teacher means it's less important
- rush! Consult widely and involve everyone who has a voice, especially those whose jobs are likely to be affected
- make someone take on levels of responsibility they feel unable to cope with. Not everyone feels able to take on new challenges – they're perfectly happy with the way things are. And sometimes, that's OK
- underestimate the fear of change
- get despondent if the change process is slow.

Source: NRT website.

CONCLUSION

In conclusion, it must be emphasized that change is a complex, long-term and non-linear process, not a simple one-off event. In-depth and lasting change involves alterations in people's attitudes, values and beliefs, and hence in the culture of the school. Because of this, change is destabilizing, often threatening for individuals and groups involved, and therefore frequently involves conflict. For these reasons rational models are inadequate for understanding and managing the change process.

The next chapter considers the first step in managing any change: finding out what needs changing as a result of auditing the current state of affairs.

Chapter 4

How do you spend your worktime?

- The ATL worktime audit
- How to complete the audit
- The pilot
- Collective auditing

Teachers currently have few tools to help judge whether the deployment of their time is contributing to the raising of standards and whether the position is getting better or worse, and none that cover both together. This chapter is about how teachers use their time. It describes the development of an audit we devised in 2002–03 – funded by the Association of Teachers and Lecturers (ATL) – which has been used by teachers to ascertain how they are currently deploying their time, with a view to seeing whether that time is being used effectively, especially in relation to their own development and that of their pupils.

THE ATL WORKTIME AUDIT

Individual teachers can benefit from auditing their use of time. This enables them to see how they are spending time, consider the value of spending it on certain tasks and activities, and if necessary think about how they can achieve any changes in their practice. Auditing use of time could be used in any or all of the following ways:

- monitor use of time to check efficiency and effectiveness
- as hard evidence for individuals to discuss their workload with their line managers
- to inform performance management.

The aim of the ATL project was to design, pilot and evaluate an audit suitable for use by an individual classroom teacher in primary and secondary schools. The intention was to develop a framework of indicators for an individual teacher which:

- would prompt useful reflection from a single application (which includes a personal action plan)

- would be suitable for repeated application to detect and report trends

- would meet personal objectives for enhancing teaching quality and overall professionalism.

The ATL teachers' worktime audit is divided into four different sections:

1   A diary for each of the seven days in a week, categorizing time spent on all work in and outside school.

2   A daily summary to say what activities gave the most and least value for the pupils and professional satisfaction.

3   A summary of the week – collating use of time and comparing it with teachers in the 2003 STRB survey.

4   Drawing up an action plan of how to change an aspect of worktime.

The audit takes between 15 and 30 minutes a day to complete. Most teachers completed it once a day ('in the evening, as there is little time in the day'). It did take time and, of course, in the short term, added to teachers' workload but, as one teacher who had found the use of the audit helpful noted, it is about 'taking time to make time'!

In its analyses of teachers' workload, the School Teachers' Review Body (STRB) made use of categories of activities and asked teachers to use them to undertake a diary exercise of their use of time. In order for meaningful comparisons to be made with the work of the STRB, we used compatible categories of grouped activities. They are:

- teaching

- cover and registration

- lesson preparation and classroom organization

- marking and assessment

- non-teaching contact with pupils and parents

- school/staff management

- administrative tasks

- professional development.

A more detailed breakdown of the above categories is given in Table 4.1. The next section gives guidance on how to complete the worktime audit we devised.

HOW TO COMPLETE THE AUDIT

1 Running record (Table 4.2)

Use the running record each day for a week (including the weekend) to note down how long is spent on the above categories. Please refer to the more detailed breakdown of the categories in Table 4.1 when deciding the type of activity. Each day's record should cover all time at school and any work done outside school. There is an example in Table 4.3. You will probably find it easiest if you complete the record at some convenient points in the day (e.g. break, lunchtime). It is important for you to have an accurate picture of how you have deployed your time. If you find that two or more activities are occurring simultaneously (e.g. your teaching is interrupted by a parent's visit) make a note but record the main activity only.

2 Summary of the day (Table 4.4)

This asks for two things for each day:

1   Add up the minutes spent on each category onto the summary of the day sheet.

2   Then consider each day's work, in terms of:

(a) the value for the pupils of the various activities

(b) the degree of professional satisfaction you have derived from undertaking them.

Simply adding up the amount of time you spend on tasks tells you nothing about how exhausted or frustrated certain tasks leave you. For instance, in terms of stress the 15 minutes spent dealing with disruptive pupils or ten minutes unjamming the photocopier may feel equal to an hour's planning.

3 Summary of your week (Table 4.5)

At the end of your week, collate all your time spent on the categories each day and put them into the Benchmark sheets.

Table 4.1	The job of a teacher broken down into grouped activities

Teaching (T)

T1. Own lesson/teaching/tutorial

T2. Assisting pupils in other people's lessons

T3. Educational visit

Cover and registration (C)

C1. Covering absent teacher's lesson

C2. Registration/general classroom management/pastoral/counselling session

C3. Administering test/invigilating exam

Preparation of lesson and classroom (P)

P1. Planning/preparing lesson, practical test or assessment (incl. gathering materials)

P2. Displaying/mounting pupils' work or information for pupils

P3. Setting up/tidying classroom, lab or other teaching area

P4. Other non-contact activities relating to a lesson or class

Marking and assessment (M)

M1. Marking pupil work (including exam/test)

M2. Keeping records on pupil performance (e.g. for National Curriculum, school records, examination boards)

M3. Writing reports on pupil progress (e.g. end of term report)

Non-teaching contact with pupils and parents (N)

N1. Supervising pupils before/during/after pupil day (e.g. during breaks, assembly)

N2. Coaching sport, rehearsing drama/music or organizing pupil clubs/societies (not as part of timetabled teaching)

N3. Disciplining/praising pupils

N4. Pastoral care with individual pupils

N5. Any contact with parents/families (incl. PTA meetings and parents' evenings)

N6. Other non-teaching activities relating to particular pupils or parents

School/staff management (S)

S1. Any staff meeting (including preparation, writing agenda/minutes etc.)

S2. Appraising teaching staff and monitoring lessons

S3. Contact with teaching staff

S4. Arranging teaching duties, timetables, pupil allocation or supply

S5. Contact with support staff (including management/supervision)

S6. School policy development (including planning, implementation)

S7. Financial management and planning (incl. money-raising events)

S8. Contact with governors

S9. Contact with educational bodies

S10. Other management related activities

Administrative tasks (A)

A1. Simple clerical activity (e.g. photocopying, filing, routine form filling/database entry)

A2. Keeping records or department records (excluding those on pupil performances)

A3. Organizing resources and premises (e.g. buildings, equipment, books, computers)

A4. Other kinds of administrative activities

Professional development activity (D)

D1. Training other staff (including teachers, NQTs, students and associate staff)

D2. Being trained or appraised (e.g. attending training course, INSET)

D3. Studying/background reading (excluding preparing for particular lessons)

D4. Keeping this self audit

D5. Other individual/professional activity

Other (O)

Authorized absence during school hours

Source: Bubb et al., 2003, based on STRB 2003.

| Table 4.2 | Running record of how you spend your worktime (*photocopy one sheet for each day including the weekend*) |

Date:

Time	Duration in minutes	Code	Work activity

Managing Teacher Workload © Sara Bubb and Peter Earley 2004

| Table 4.3 | Example of running record | | |

Time	Duration in minutes	Code	Work activity
7.50 – 8.00	10	S3	Speak to Senco
8.00 – 8.15	15	A1	Photocopying
8.15 – 8.45	20 10	P3 P2	Setting up room and display
8.45 – 8.55	10	S1	Morning meeting
8.55 – 9.05	10	C2	Register
9.05 – 10.15	70	T1	Teaching
10.15 – 10.30	15	N1	Assembly – attended
10.30 – 10.50	20	N1	Playtime – on duty
10.50 – 12.00	70	T1	Teaching
12.00 – 12.10	10	N3	Kept 3 children in
12.10 – 1.00	20 30	P3 S3	Lunch – tidying, setting up Talking to other staff
1.00 – 1.10	10	C2	Register
1.10 – 3.00	110	T1	Teaching
3.00 – 3.15	15	N5	Home time, chat to parents
3.15 – 3.45	30	P3	Tidying
3.45 – 5.00	75	S1	Staff meeting
5.00 – 5.15	15	A1	Sorted work
5.15 – 5.50			Travelled home
5.50 – 7.30			Domestic
7.30 – 8.00	30	M1	Marking
8.30 – 9.00	60	P1	Planning. Cut out resources for tomorrow's lesson
Various	20	D4	Doing this audit

Source: Bubb et al. 2003.

| Table 4.4 | Daily summary (*photocopy one sheet for each day including the weekend*) |

Date:

Part 1: Worktime

Type of activity *	Teaching (T)	Cover & register (C)	Lesson prep & org (P)	Marking & assess (M)	Non-teaching contact (N)	Sch/staff manag (S)	Admin (A)	Prof devt (D)	Other (O)
Collate mins									
Total mins									

*Please see Table 4.1 for a detailed breakdown of each type of work activity

Part 2: Worktime – value and satisfaction

Please comment on the work you have undertaken in terms of a) its value to the pupils, and, b) the degree of professional satisfaction gained.

Value of activity

Which activity has given:

   most value to the pupils?

   least value to the pupils?

Professional satisfaction

Which activity has given you:

   most professional satisfaction?

   least professional satisfaction?

   most stress or frustration?

Managing Teacher Workload © Sara Bubb and Peter Earley 2004

Table 4.5	Benchmark yourself against other teachers, working hours

Grouped activities	Yours	Average primary teacher	Average secondary teacher	+ or -
Teaching (T) total		18h 48m	18h 36m	
T1. Own lesson/teaching/tutorial		18h 6m	17h 54m	
T2. Assisting pupils in other people's lessons		18m	18m	
T3. Educational visit		24m	24m	
Cover & registration (C)		1h 42m	2h 42m	
C1. Covering a lesson		6m	48m	
C2. Registration/classroom management/pastoral		1h 30m	1h 36m	
C3. Administering test/exam		6m	18m	
Lesson prep & classroom org. (P)		12h 42m	7h 42m	
P1. Planning/preparing lesson		8h 12m	5h 48m	
P2. Display		1h	12m	
P3. Setting up/tidying classroom, etc.		2h 48m	1h 6m	
P4. Other non-contact tasks relating to a lesson		42m	36m	
Marking & assessment (M)		5h 24m	8h 30m	
M1. Marking pupil work (including exam/test)		4h 12m	6h 24m	
M2. Keeping records on pupil performance		54m	36m	
M3. Writing reports on pupil progress		18m	1h 30m	
Non-teaching contact with pupils/parents (N)		4h 54m	5h 18m	
N1. Supervising pupils		2h 30m	1h 18m	
N2. Coaching, rehearsing, clubs/societies		36m	1h 18m	
N3. Disciplining/praising pupils		12m	36m	
N4. Pastoral care with individual pupils		6m	30m	
N5. Contact with parents/families		1h	54m	
N6. Other non-teaching of pupils or parents		24m	42m	

Table 4.5 continued

Grouped activities	Yours	Average primary teacher	Average secondary teacher	+ or -
School/staff management (S)		4h 12m	3h 18m	
S1. Any staff meeting		1h 30m	1h 18m	
S2. Appraising/ monitoring teachers		6m	6m	
S3. Training other staff		12m	12m	
S4. Contact with other teachers		1h	48m	
S5. Arranging teaching duties, timetables		6m	18m	
S6. Contact with support staff		12m	6m	
S7. School policy development		30m	6m	
S8. Financial man't & planning		6m	*	
S9. Contact with governors		6m	*	
S10. Contact with educational bodies		6m	6m	
S11. Other management activities		18m	18m	
Administrative tasks (A) total		1h 36m	2h	
A1. Simple clerical activity		36m	42m	
A2. Keeping records or department records		12m	18m	
A3. Organizing resources and premises		30m	30m	
A4. Other kinds of admin activities		18m	30m	
Professional devt activity (D) total		3h 6m	2h 36m	
D1. Being trained or appraised		1h6m	48m	
D2. Studying/background reading		30m	30m	
D3. Keeping this audit		54m	42m	
D4. Other professional activity		36m	36m	
TOTAL working hours		52h 24m	50h 48m	

4 Analyse your worktime and draw up an action plan (Table 4.6)

Compare your use of time with the STRB survey results. Remember that their tables are just averages and disguise a wide variation. For instance, although primary teachers on average worked some 52 hours in the survey week, nearly 20 per cent worked over 60 hours and around 5 per cent did under 40 hours. You also need to consider how typical your week was. Do you normally work:

- longer hours
- shorter hours, or
- about the same as this week?

If the week wasn't typical, think why.

Bearing in mind the above, look particularly at those tasks on which you spend more (and less) time than the STRB survey average. You might want to use the last column to calculate how much more or less you worked. An analysis of your daily running record will give you more detail of exactly how you are spending your time within the various work activity headings. For instance, if you're unhappy with how long you are spending on 'Lesson preparation and classroom organization' you could look at the running records to ascertain which of the elements – planning/preparing lessons; display; or setting up/tidying classroom – are more time-consuming.

Now that you have the big picture of how you spend your time, and the comparison with other teachers, how do you feel about the way you are making use of your time? Take account of your daily records in which you noted the tasks that:

- were of most and least value to the pupils
- gave most and least professional satisfaction
- caused most stress and frustration.

What do you want to change?

Consider:

1   What things are achievable by you alone?

2   What will need to change at a school organization level? All teachers will soon have planning, preparation and admin (PPA) time, but what other changes would be useful?

How are you going to change an element of your worktime? Draw up an action plan of how you are going to achieve the change in worktime.

Table 4.6 A worktime action plan

Date:

What I'm going to spend less time on:

How long do I spend on it at the moment?

How many minutes am I going to save?   By when?

How I'm going to do it, who's involved	When	Record any time reduction and other comments

Review notes

Managing Teacher Workload © Sara Bubb and Peter Earley

- What do you want to spend less time on?

- How are you going to do so? What implications are there for others?

- How much time are you going to save, and by when? Are you aiming for a radical or a gradual reduction?

- How are you going to measure your progress?

- How will you spend the time saved? It shouldn't be spent on more work-related tasks!

Cost–benefit analysis

It's useful to analyse the cost–benefit of someone else doing a task rather than you. The school workforce agreement has encouraged this. Think of something that could be done by someone else such as playground duty, photocopying, tidying, taking the register and use the questions in Table 4.7 to think about what you could delegate.

THE PILOT

The project was divided into two phases:

Phase 1

1 We designed a worktime audit and a booklet of suggestions for reducing worktime.

2 Twenty teachers offered to try the audit over a week in late October/early November 2002 and to write an action plan of how they would reduce an aspect of their workload.

3 We interviewed them about how they found the process and discussed their action plan.

4 We revised the audit in the light of teacher feedback.

Phase 2

5 Teachers tried out the revised audit in mid-February 2003 to see whether their worktime had decreased.

6 We interviewed them about how they found the process.

We aimed to find 20 teachers who were ATL members in ten different schools (two per school). Finding teachers willing to be involved in piloting the audit, however, was hard. This in itself is evidence of how teachers feel about their work, that they felt they were too busy to take on anything more. Eventually, 20 teachers spread across 12 schools (six primary and six secondary) agreed to take part in the project.

Table 4.7 Cost–benefit analysis

Task	
What's the cost of you doing the task?	
Cost of support staff doing it?	
Benefit of you doing it, as opposed to support staff?	
What else could you be doing in that time?	
How does doing that task affect other things you have to do?	
Who could do the task?	
How much time will be spent explaining the task?	
What are the risks involved in them doing the task?	

Three of the 20 teachers did not carry out the Phase 1 audit – one because of illness and two because of time factors. Of the 17 who were involved in Phase 1, only eight people – less than half – completed the audit a term later. The reasons for the drop-out rate were various: one had left the ATL, two were facing an Ofsted inspection, one had a student teacher and didn't feel that the audit week would be typical, and some were ill or on paternity leave. One person saw no point in doing the audit again: 'The first time I thought it was a miracle way of reducing workload but as this didn't happen and I knew it wasn't going to happen, I felt disillusioned.'

What we found

As noted above at the end of both phase 1 and phase 2 of the project we conducted interviews with the primary and secondary school teachers who trialed the audit. How were they spending their time and what aspects of their work do they consider to be of most value to pupils, most professionally satisfying and most stressful, and why?

Teachers worked for different lengths of time and spent their week in different ways. For instance, the special needs co-ordinator of a middle school who was paid on the Upper Pay Scale and had three management points worked for 63 hours. She spent 24 per cent of her time teaching but 30 per cent in preparing, organizing, marking and assessing. A secondary deputy head spent 21 per cent of his time in supervising and disciplining pupils – and felt very little job satisfaction because of this. Table 4.8 shows how four teachers spent their time.

Table 4.8 **How different teachers spent their time in one week (percentages)**

	2ndry deputy (61 hrs)	Senco (63 hrs)	Prim ind tutor (51 hrs)	NQT (56 hrs)
Teaching	14	24	37	35
Preparation and organization	6	14	11	17
Marking and assessment	2	16	6	9
Non-teaching – parents and pupils	21	20	3	17
Management	45 (including 14% providing prof devt)	10	18	4
Admin	11	8	6	3
Prof devt	1	5	18	16
Total	100	100	100	100

Bubb et al., 2003

Some teachers spent a high proportion of their time on administrative tasks that could perhaps have been done by a member of the support staff. One head of department wrote of the frustration of having to spend nearly seven hours in one week checking and collating reports. She had to correct other teachers' mistakes (spelling and grammar) and had to check through wrong attendance data.

It was interesting to see when teachers did their work. The secondary deputy head worked 13-hour days (7.30 a.m. until 8.30 p.m.) at school for four days, only leaving 'early' (5 p.m., after nine hours' work) on Friday. One secondary head of year arrived at school at 7.50 a.m. and didn't leave until 6.45 p.m. except on the Wednesday when he left at 5.30 p.m. He appeared to do all his marking at the weekend – two and a half hours on Saturday and one and a half hours on Sunday. He spent two more hours on Sunday planning lessons and assemblies. Thus he had no days that were work-free. Most teachers did school work on at least one day over the weekend. Several teachers left school at about 5 p.m. but then spent two or three more hours working in the evening at home.

Several teachers pointed out that the STRB codes and categories did not show or adequately reflect the multi-tasking (e.g. photocopying while talking to the special needs co-ordinator and being interrupted by a pupil, while trying to drink a cup of coffee) that is such a common feature of teachers' lives – and is so tiring and stressful. The nature of a teacher's job is that so many tasks and activities are undertaken, sometimes simultaneously, and it was difficult to reduce these without detracting from an accurate picture of how the working day is spent. Some found it difficult to code certain activities – 'my SEN [special educational needs] admin: is it A4 or S10?'. Several teachers' working hours were greater than were accounted for using the categories. For instance, one was certain that she had been at school or working at home for 73 hours but her recorded activities added up to 63 hours. This may indicate that time just disappears particularly in talking to colleagues but not about specific things that could be fitted under the listed categories.

Our audit does not show the levels of intensity of certain activities. To do so, teachers could colour-code their running record highlighting high stress activities (teaching certain lessons, dealing with difficult pupils or parents) in red, medium stress activities in yellow and low stress ones (perhaps preparing resources, or planning at home) in green.

Participants varied in how useful they thought it was to consider what aspects of the job gave satisfaction. Some found it helped to prioritize tasks. One said, 'it was good to reflect on the day's experiences, remembering the positive bits!' and it was 'interesting to see when least value to students and stress coincide'. Where teachers found it less useful, it was because the same was being recorded every day 'and everything is ultimately of use to the children'. Another said:

> I think these headings are all useful in trying to prioritize tasks. I should concentrate on value to pupils, as that is why I originally went into teaching. However pressure from

outside agencies, government reforms, the head, the LEA and staff means that I'll personally look to the professional satisfaction to judge my success. Frustration is usually down to time and having to settle for a sliding scale of success: 80 per cent now down to 'if I do a half good job that is good enough'. This is a worrying slippery slope.

More effective use of time?

We found that worktime was reduced for most of the teachers, though they were not sure whether the reduction was genuine or because it was just a different week. They were concerned that no two weeks are the same, which makes comparisons hard. However, it was interesting to see that the trend was towards working time being reduced! Table 4.9 shows some participants' working hours for both the Phase 1 and 2 weeks. It is also interesting to note the range of hours worked, from about 42 hours to over 65 hours per week, and the relationship between length of the working week and position in school.

Table 4.9	Examples of worktime changes		
	Phase 1 week	*Phase 2 week*	*Difference*
SENCO	64 hr 45 min	63 hr 20 min	-1 hr 25 min
Leadership group	61 hr	65 hr 18 min	+4 hr 18 min
Mainscale KS3 co-ord	53 hr	42 hr 20 min	-10 hr 40 min
Acting deputy head	51 hr	51 hr 35 min	+35 min
KS4 science +3	62 hr 25 min	54 hr	-8 hr 35 min
Mainscale +2	50 hr	48 hr 45 min	-1 hr 15 min
Mainscale +1	45 hr 50 min	45 hr 35 min	-15 min
HoD	42 hr 55 min	41 hr 40 min	-1 hr 15 min

Bubb et al., 2003

Many teachers did think they could use their time more efficiently. However, it was deemed difficult 'because you often start one thing and then you get sucked into other things' or 'I cannot see much space for time saving apart from being quicker using IT'. Another remarked how the job was becoming professionally unrewarding noting that fewer activities were being done to the standard she would like to achieve. 'I am forever compromising on quality or half completing tasks.' For another the result of completing the Phase 1 autumn term's workload diary had made her realize that she was spending far too much time on marking.

Teachers reported making a number of changes to their worktime (e.g. less photocopying) but matters were often complicated by taking on new roles (e.g. 'I have recently taken on the role of acting deputy. So I am now Deputy Head, full time class teacher, literacy co-coordinator and in charge of school visits. As Deputy Head I am assessment, curriculum and professional development coordinator – and I only have half a day non-contact time a week'). Others were trying to prioritize their work a bit more and to be more realistic about what could be achieved but a crucial issue was what was or was not in their control. For example:

I don't see how changing my work practice would decrease my workload. Areas that cause stress and frustration and where I spend a lot of my time are areas that I cannot exert any influence on. My job is a series of spinning plates on poles and the only way to perhaps reduce them is to drop one. The way that is decided is what are the repercussions of dropping a particular plate as opposed to another one.

Teachers found it difficult to quantify how much time they had saved but some were able to put a figure on it – 'Marking time (by about three hours)'; 'less photocopying (about one hour)'.

● Bringing about change

Is the voluntary use of an audit tool beneficial in bringing about change and greater job satisfaction and work-life balance? The answer to this question is both yes – and no!

Teachers gave examples as to how they had altered their work patterns; e.g. reorganize storage of SEN paperwork; using different marking procedures; marking coursework in less detail; less photocopying. The changes were generally considered to be positive and in one case the changes had created more time to talk to colleagues and share ideas. For another it was:

Really useful to focus on what I do and then look at the benchmark to see where I am spending more time than average so I can focus on cutting down my workload in that area. Before the audit I knew I was spending a lot of time marking, but the audit forced me to focus on this area and it was good that it went hand in hand with the suggestions booklet because having identified marking as an area where I was perhaps spending too much time, I was then able to look at practical suggestions on how to reduce this.

Some people had increased their worktime but this was because their role had changed or they had taken on additional responsibilities e.g. teaching booster classes for SATs; an increase in marking because of a school initiative; and leading the KS3 strategy. For some the extra work was difficult to quantify, others were quite specific (e.g. '2 x 1 hour sessions after school each week'). The extra work meant that there was less time for other things, not much time to talk to colleagues and a need to prioritize ('I can't do everything'). The time increase was also affecting life outside school, with the need to do more work in the evenings and longer hours in school, leaving less time for their own families.

COLLECTIVE AUDITING

The audit can be used by individuals at any time but it might be particularly beneficial when workload is perceived to be getting too great or when new roles have been taken on. Our research found that teachers enjoyed being able to talk through their audit and compare their use of time with others, so work in pairs is useful. It needs, wherever possible, to be a collective act.

The big drawback however – and an unsurprising one – is that there is a limit to how much change to their work practices an individual or pairs of individuals can make. Our respondents felt frustrated because they felt there needed to be changes at a *whole-school level*, in order for them to alter how they were spending their worktime. Structural and organizational factors were preventing further change occurring. This, of course, is where the workforce remodelling programme will help.

It is ideal for teams or the whole staff to complete the audit and discuss the common areas of concern. This means that results can be compared with colleagues in the same context. Another advantage is that there would be greater awareness and evidence of significant 'time' issues – 'where are we spending the bulk of our time and why?' – and it would give individuals power to initiate change at the level of the whole school or department. For instance, teachers in an English department could compare their use of time, and perhaps look particularly at how they manage marking, etc.

Some matters would come to the attention of school managers as requiring immediate attention as they were seen as a major source of 'time-wasting' and, perhaps more importantly, stress and frustration. It may be that getting the entire staff to complete the audit to discover that a major cause of stress and ineffective use of time is the malfunctioning photocopier or a poorly resourced staffroom is a little excessive, but it may be the only way that something gets done! The undertaking of the audit in this manner may mean that action is finally taken to rectify a problem that clearly has not been given the priority it deserves.

Teams or all staff in schools or groups of schools could complete the audit and discuss findings at an in-service education and training (INSET) day. Benchmarking or comparing results with people in different schools might encourage the spreading of good practice, creative thinking and, for some schools, the radical change that might be part of the remodelling the workforce initiative.

We can all work more effectively – by managing to ensure things work well and that people feel valued and professionally satisfied. The audit could be used to this end. However, several of the teachers in our small sample found the results of the audit depressing because it made clear to them the impossibility of doing their job well in the situations they currently found themselves. To avoid negative consequences, teachers need to be encouraged to:

- look at what they're doing well

- see how efficient they are in using time

- decide what needs to be prioritized and changed.

This should not be an isolated activity but, rather, data derived from the audit can be used as a basis for discussion about wider school issues. If the audit isn't linked to opportunities for change where necessary, teachers may feel bitter or disillusioned on two counts: that they are powerless to remedy situations and that they have wasted precious time in doing the audit for no reason. In order to help reduce this, consideration has to be given to wider school issues, particularly staffing and management of resources. For example, consideration may be given to the Healthy Schools initiative and related attempts at enhancing staff wellbeing and work-life balance, such as the Well-Being Programme (see Chapter 2). Also as we saw in Chapter 2, the school workforce or remodelling agreement is also introducing changes some of which are contractual.

CONCLUSION

In the light of the remodelling agreement there is a real need to explore further the use of teachers' time and, importantly, to link this to job satisfaction and staff wellbeing. A happy and professionally satisfied member of staff is more likely to be a better teacher with obvious implications for pupils' learning. However, individual teacher responses to workload issues help only to marginalize the issue – of course we can all get better at what we do and use our time more effectively – but unless workload concerns are considered at a structural or organizational level then little progress is likely to occur. The effective deployment and use of the school's resources, especially its people resource, is the responsibility of headteachers, governing bodies and other school leaders. Individual teachers' responses to workload issues are likely to be useful but limited unless wider school issues are considered. The government's remodelling agreement is increasingly forcing schools to consider these broader concerns.

Chapter 5

How do you take care of yourself – and others?

- Work-life balance
- Time management
- Managing stress
- Make your school a better place to work in

Research tells us that those who become teachers do so for a number of reasons, of which the most important is often related to the children and being involved in their growth and development. Those entering teaching do so mainly for intrinsic reasons, though extrinsic factors play a part (Edmonds et al., 2002). Teachers and headteachers rarely put their own needs in front of others – they are not good at looking after themselves! This chapter argues that it is important to consider your own welfare and wellbeing if for no other reason that the children are not going to get a good deal from a tired, stressed, overworked teacher who works in a 'dysfunctional' and poorly managed and led school. We all know that to give of our best we need to be primed and raring to go! Our students certainly can detect when we are not looking after ourselves because it is often expressed in the quality of our work. So what do we need to consider? This chapter discusses issues around work-life balance, time management, managing stress and how to make your school a better place in which to work.

WORK-LIFE BALANCE

Wherever you're working, it's useful to see how you spend your time. Complete Table 5.1 for one week to get a feel for whether you have a work-life balance. 'Me time' should include anything that you feel better for, such as socializing, going out, exercise, watching a favourite television programme, reading, soaking in the

Table 5.1   How do you spend your time? (Bubb, 2004a, p. 96)

	Working at school	Working at home	Travel	Domestic	'Me' time	Sleep
Sun						
Mon						
Tues						
Weds						
Thurs						
Fri						
Sat						
Total						

bath, talking to someone you like. Under 'domestic' put basic everyday living – cooking, shopping, tidying, washing, cleaning, talking to people at home, eating.

You don't have to be precise in allocating time, but does each day add up roughly to 24 hours? If it's under, maybe you, like most of us, find that time just disappears. This is lovely if you're on holiday – in fact it's one of the marks of a relaxed day when you can't think what you've done with your time … and don't care. When you're a teacher though, disappearing hours can be dangerous because there's just too much to do and you'll get behind.

Look at your chart (Table 5.1). What are you doing too little of? If you don't get enough *sleep*, noisy classrooms are unbearable and you're likely to become run down, so that's a definite one to keep an eye on. If you don't spend enough time on domestic matters you may feel your life is spiralling into chaos.

Travel

Is there anyway that travel time or the stress that it engenders can be reduced by, say, going to work before the morning rush hour and leaving before the evening one starts? If you use public transport, could you get anything done in travel time – marking, planning, thinking, some 'me' time reading, or a quick nap? Perhaps you can see your journey as a good way to wind down after a day's work, almost like a rite of passage. One teacher returned to her old job that had a long journey because the new one was so close that there seemed to be no gap between work and home, so she had no winding-down time. For those of you with dependants at home, travelling may be the only time you get to yourself.

Work

What are you doing too much of? Working at *work*? Working at home? It's useful to benchmark yourself against others. For instance, as we explained in Chapter 1, the STRB (2003) survey found that although primary teachers on average work some 52 hours in term time, 16 per cent work over 60 hours and around 6 per cent under 40 hours. Secondary heads of department work 52.7 hours but 8 per cent work less than 40 hours a week and 23 per cent work for over 60 hours. How can you make savings? This chapter might give you some ideas or do the audit in Chapter 4 to get a detailed picture of how you spend your time.

Perhaps you feel perfectly happy with the length of time you spend working (though the very fact that you're reading this book renders this unlikely). Even those people who work very long hours sometimes feel happy with their lot. If you enjoy your work and it becomes like a hobby, then why not spend a lot of time on it?

But what about other people's views of your work-life balance? Do your family and friends feel short-changed? If they do, this will cause problems sooner or later, so address the issues. Perhaps this means you changing so that you do spend more time with them or maybe you need to explain the pros and cons of your work to them. For instance, the benefit of bringing work home is that you are home for your family and the alternative is that you stay at work longer. Your income, from which they benefit, means that you have to work hard. Your intensive work in some weeks balances with being around for your family for the holidays. Perhaps we as teachers are too giving – and the more we give, the more people expect. So, be assertive and state your case so that your family and friends understand things from your point of view.

'Me' time

Everyone needs some 'me' time to make their life feel more than just work. Interests outside work really help keep everything in perspective. These may be as simple as meeting friends, eating good meals, exercise or just making quiet time for yourself. Proper 'hobbies' are good too – something to stretch you in a different direction and introduce you to new people and ideas. Make it regular – something to look forward to and that you keep doing.

Domestic

Are there chores that someone else can do or are there short-cuts to be made? Too often we think that if we do chores they are 'free' but obviously they're not if we price up our time and think about what else we could be doing. Look at the economics: isn't the £5 spent on getting the shopping delivered through an Internet order worth the time, effort and hassle saved going to the supermarket? A professional decorator and general handyman generally charge less than your hourly rate and will probably get jobs done quicker and better than you. And can you put a price on the feeling that you have when you return home to a clean house or tidy garden?

TIME MANAGEMENT

Perhaps one of the best tips for managing your time is to keep track of how you spend it, perhaps by using the audit we discussed in Chapter 4. Review how much time you wasted on unimportant matters and tasks you should have delegated. Then try to work smarter not harder. Think about the quality of your time, as well as the quantity available. It's worth recognizing which part of the day – or night – is the most productive for you – the time when you have your most creative ideas, or can concentrate best. For the majority of people this is early in the day, when they are freshest. A minority of people do their best work late at night.

About 20 per cent of our time is prime time and, used well, it should produce about 80 per cent of our most creative and productive work. So use the time at school before teaching commences to get something demanding done rather than fritter away time chatting and photocopying. We know three teachers who get into school at 6 a.m. but just sit and chat, which is not a good use of time. Leave such things till you're too tired to do anything else. The rest of your time is likely to be of lower quality, and is nowhere near as productive. In this low quality time, plan to do things that are easy to pick up after interruptions or jobs that you look forward to doing.

If you work without decent breaks your effectiveness will be diminished. Few of us have an opportunity to take a siesta but, whether or not we can take a nap, there is still a natural tendency for our energy levels to dip in the afternoon. We usually have to override the low energy period with adrenalin in order to teach effectively, but this then builds up a debt of doziness for later. The debt is repaid the moment we sit down to think, mark, plan, or arrive at an end-of-day meeting. This is not high-quality time. There is not always a lot we can do about this, but, being aware of it, we can sometimes plan our non-teaching commitments in alternative ways.

Lesson planning, writing reports (see Chapter 6) and other difficult jobs need high-quality time. If you try to do them at times when you'll be interrupted, or are tired and hungry you'll become frustrated, and everything will take longer. You also need to consider where you work best:

> *I just get so annoyed that being in the building seems to equate in so many people's minds with being committed. It seems to me that most of it is mere presentism. Am I alone in finding that I work far more efficiently at home where I am not surrounded by others and can focus much more efficiently on lesson preparation, marking or admin?*
>
> (NQT, quoted in Bubb, 2004, p. 104)

It seems to be the done thing in primary schools at least to stay as long as possible - there's definitely a competitive element to it. There are teachers who came in at 7 or 7.30 a.m. and stay until 5.30 p.m. or later, and still go home with huge amounts of work. Let's face it, if you're a teacher who cares even a little bit about the quality of work you do, you will be investing massive amounts of your own time on the job outside directed hours. Indeed, you could work all the time if you were so inclined and still have more things to do: evenings, weekends, holidays. There's always room for work, but you need a life too. Remember that a tired teacher is rarely an effective teacher so you need to be at your best between the school's core hours – 9 to 4.

How to work smarter not harder

You may have some routine matters to attend to, or some longer-term issues. Whatever the task, it's best to break it into bite-sized chunks by using the acronym SMART. This is usually used in relation to target-setting – for both pupils and teachers – but we can use it here to think about the tasks we do and to make them more 'do-able'.

Specific, clearly defined.

Measurable, so that it's easy to see when it has been completed.

Attainable – unrealistic tasks are depressing, as we can't achieve them.

Relevant, or appropriate, to current and future needs.

Time-limited with defined deadlines – open-ended tasks have a habit of not getting done.

If each task that we plan is examined according to SMART criteria, it will be easier to achieve, and there is nothing better for reducing stress than the confidence borne of success!

Here are some more suggestions for how to manage your time well:

- List what needs to be done, deciding how much time to devote to each task and setting realistic deadlines. Set interim deadlines for major projects like reports working back from the deadline (see Table 6.4 in Chapter 6). Both of us use our diaries in this way – it's so lovely when you cross things off your list!

- Prioritize – you might use an A, B, C approach where A represents the urgent, B the important and C the things that can safely be put on one side. Don't waste time procrastinating. Chapter 8 contains some more ideas for prioritizing tasks and how to recognize when you're procrastinating.

- Focus on doing and, if possible, completing one task at a time. This is hard to do in a school but if you juggle too many balls you are likely to drop them all. Avoid overloading yourself. Build in rewards for tasks you don't like doing.

- When do you work best? Fit work around energy highs and lows. Save tasks that don't require much concentration for the low spots in your day, e.g. do simple jobs like photocopying (if you haven't delegated them) before you leave for the day rather than at the start of the next, when you're at your freshest.

- Set boundaries for school work – not just in terms of time, but also quality and quantity. The same task might take one or three hours to complete depending on how much time you allow. The questions to ask are, 'Is it really any better at the end of three hours, and does it need to be this good?' Is a Rolls Royce needed or will a Ford Fiesta do just as well? Accept what is 'good enough'.

- Get rid of distractions as far as possible. Be firm with yourself and those around you. Avoid stressful people and those who sap your energy and eat up your time – the time bandits!

MANAGING STRESS

What is stress?

The Health and Safety Executive (HSE) define stress as 'the adverse reaction people have to excessive pressures or other types of demand placed upon them. It arises when they worry they can't cope'. Stress is 'an excess of perceived demands over an individual's perceived ability to meet them' (TSN, 2002 p. 1). Pressure in itself is not necessarily bad and many people thrive on it but stress is complex – there is good stress (eustress) and bad stress (distress) as well as too much (hyperstress) and not enough (hypostress). It is when pressure is experienced as excessive by an individual that poor health and stress-related illness could result. It is complicated, however, by the fact that stress affects different people in different ways – staff doing the same task in the same setting respond to 'stressors' differently! It is crucial for schools to be aware of this especially in the light of recent legal decisions.

In a landmark decision in 2004, the House of Lords ruled that employers must take the initiative to protect employees once they know that an individual is vulnerable to stress-related illness. Alan Barber of East Bridgwater Secondary School was awarded £72,547 plus interest and costs against his employers, Somerset County Council.

Mr Barber's illness started in 1995. At that time he was responsible for the mathematics department and carried a full teaching load. In addition, he took responsibility for publicity and public relations at a time when the school was determined to improve its image and attract more pupils. The two roles, combined with the removal of his deputies, meant that Mr Barber was regularly working between 61 and 70 hours a week and he began to suffer stress at work. In May 1996 his doctor signed him off sick for depression brought on by the heavy workload. Despite his complaints to the senior management at his school about the pressure he was under, nothing was done to improve his situation. He eventually found it pointless to complain further. He became seriously ill in November 1996 and has not worked since.

Doug McAvoy, NUT General Secretary, said: 'This is a most significant ruling and restores responsibility where it belongs. Teachers endure excessive workload and are subject to continuous monitoring. Teaching is a most stressful profession. Teachers need and deserve all the support necessary to protect their health.' The judgement overturned an earlier decision of the Court of Appeal which had been understood as placing the onus on the employee to ensure that the employer is kept fully informed. Being aware of stress and how the school may be creating it is therefore essential. Poor management is certainly a factor (see Chapter 8) but research has shown that certain work-related factors emerge as common causes of stress amongst teachers (see Figure 5.1).

Figure 5.1	Work-related factors causing stress

Common themes included:
- *Relationships with pupils* – e.g.changes in pupil attitude; anxiety over tests; lack of discipline; large class size and mixed ability
- *Relationships with colleagues* – e.g. poor communication; tension and personality clashes; uneven workloads; lack of collegiality
- *Relationships with parents and wider community* – e.g. parental pressure; unrealistic expectations; increased access; general cynicism re teachers' role; media bashing
- *Innovation and change* – e.g. constant demands for change with no good reason; feelings of powerlessness and failure; rate of changes; lack of information to support and facilitate change
- *School management and administration* – poor organization and communication, lack of training to meet new demands; lack of admin support; inadequate staff facilities; poor technical back up; poor decision-making
- *Time factors* – increasing variety and number of tasks; additional work demands; frequency and ineffective organization of meetings.

Source: Brown and Ralph, 1995.

Patrick Nash, chief executive of the Teacher Support Network, says the success of the Well-Being Programme (that we discussed in Chapter 2) is that it challenges the culture of isolation that persists in many schools.

> *It's very clear that key pressures are stress over workload, the difficulties people have with colleagues and the problems with pupils. What tends to happen is that teachers deal with these in isolation. The real problem is that so often in schools there is a conspiracy of silence, where it's frowned upon to admit that you're having difficulties in the classroom, in the staff room or with a management person of your peers. It's typical workplace competition, which tends to be exaggerated in schools. Teachers work in classrooms in isolation from one another – that set-up doesn't lend itself to collegiality.*

(TSN website)

There are some signs that people in school are stressed. For example:

- more shouting, crying and irritability – more people 'losing it'

- people showing increasingly poor concentration and forgetfulness

- staff feeling tired all day and often complaining of headaches or other pains

- less humour in the staffroom

- an increase in sick leave, especially longer-term absences

- staff working longer hours, or working during breaks more frequently.

The Teacher Support Network identifies three broad areas of symptoms of stress – behaviour, and mental health and physical symptoms:

Behaviour:

- You increase your consumption of stimulants, such as alcohol or cigarettes.

- Your eating habits frequently change.

- You can become less reliable with poor timekeeping and increased absence from work and even more accident-prone.

- Personal relationships often become strained.

Mental health symptoms:

- You will often be increasingly irritable and withdrawn.

- You will suffer from anxiety and depression.

- You will usually find it harder to maintain your concentration and become increasingly forgetful.

- Sleep often becomes more difficult.

Physical symptoms:

- General aches and pains sounds almost petty, but people living with stress get tense muscles and a general lethargy.

- Digestive and blood pressure problems.

- Headaches and migraines become more frequent.

- You can become more susceptible to colds and flu.

There can be longer-term issues that develop into more complicated symptoms. Equally, any one of these points could be nothing in itself but if you recognize a number of features of your life, outlined above, then now may be a good time to identify the cause.

Coping with stress

You need to be able to cope with results of the stress and you need to begin to take steps to handle the causes. Remember, however, stress is not a weakness, and you are not failing if you feel stressed. Given that there is no one cause of stress, there can be no simple solution. Stress management is a process not a simple repair job. The first step is to recognize that the problem exists. Sharing your issues with colleagues or a family member will almost always be a good start. If your stress is work related, talk with your headteacher and union. They cannot help you unless they know a problem exists. The Teacher Support Network now offers an on-line stress assessment you can use to identify your levels of stress and then to develop strategies for coping (see TSN website). Contacting Teacher Support Line is a specific remedy open to all teachers in England and Wales. It's open every day and staffed by trained counsellors who have experience of education.

Analyse the causes of your stress. Remember that stress is not necessarily caused primarily with an event in itself, but by a concern that you have about your ability to cope with that event. You need to be very honest with yourself and face up to issues that could cause some distress. Many people swear by the idea of listing all your troubles, then dividing them into those over which you have some control, and those not. The latter you ignore and work on practical solutions to those over which you have some influence. There are usually more areas than we initially think where we can take control of our own lives.

Keep fit

This often involves doing something physical, not necessarily taking up jogging or going down the local gym. Even just a quick 20-minute walk can help and that is something you can start on today. In the slightly longer term, you should look at your diet. Watch your consumption of alcohol, cigarettes or caffeine – they may seem to help but they don't.

Relaxation

Do something that forces you to think about something other than work, something that needs your active involvement. Why not blast some aliens in a computer game rather than just having the television on in the background? Recovering from the 'high alert' positions that our bodies may have been in for long periods during the day is important and sometimes hard to do. Many of us need to learn new relaxation techniques. There is a great variety of courses, books, tapes, exercises, etc. available. Researchers at Wisconsin University monitored the brain activity of 25 randomly chosen individuals and concluded that Buddhist meditation causes a significant reduction in anxiety and correspondingly increased levels of positive emotions. They exhibited a dramatic increase in levels of activity in the prefrontal cortex, the region of the brain that is most commonly associated with wellbeing and happiness (Marsh, 2004).

Rest

Sleep is also very important and, again, there are a number of guides available to getting a good rest. A common tip is not to go to bed until you are ready, rather than at a specific time, so that you avoid too much lying awake at night. You can prepare for good quality sleep by taking a hot bath, for instance. Avoid coffee – even decaffeinated can keep you awake!

◉ Useful contacts

As well as getting help from family, friends, colleagues and your doctor you can get support from:

- The Teacher Support Network – in England call 08000 562 561 or email from the website at www.teachersupport.info. In Wales, you can call 0800 085 5088.

- Employee Assistance Programmes: these offer a range of support services, such as information, legal, financial, and face-to-face counselling. Worklife Support has tailored such services especially for the education sector.

- Well-Being Programme, which offers an ongoing framework specially designed for schools.

- Your union or professional support group will be familiar with issues relating to stress.

- Networking: meet with teachers from other schools at a similar level informally.

- The Chartered Institute of Personnel and Development for trainers and human resources specialists on 0208 971 9000 and the website at www.cipd.co.uk.

- The International Stress Management Association for stress specialists on 07000 780430 and at stress@isma.org.uk.

School responses to stress

Of course, responses to stress also need to take place at school level. What is the school doing to manage stress? Are they taking appropriate action to identify and respond to possible 'stressors'? The HSE has done a lot of research into how organizations can spot if they have a stress problem and outline some of the things that can help in a positive approach to stress reduction (see HSE, 1995; 2000). Some of the ways that schools can manage stress are outlined in Chapter 8.

MAKE YOUR SCHOOL A BETTER PLACE TO WORK IN

Employees have a right to decent working conditions and to work in a stress-free environment. Regarding the latter, some school governing bodies, conscious of the fact that they want to be seen as 'good employers', have instituted surveys of stress and its main causes within the school, with a view to doing something about rectifying them. Others have implemented significant changes to improve staff wellbeing. For instance, Grinling Gibbons is a school in Deptford, south-east London, that is heavily affected by rush-hour traffic. The start and finish times of the school day have been changed to enable staff to get to school before the worst traffic in the mornings and evenings. The school day starts at 8.30 a.m. and finishes at 2.30 p.m. There is a reduced lunchbreak and from 2.30 to 3.30 p.m. there are optional clubs, run by support staff and volunteers. In this time, staff get their planning, marking and meetings done so that everyone should be able to leave by 4 p.m.

At Two Mile Ash Middle School in Milton Keynes, the timetable is organized so that teachers have half a day off a week. And it really is time off: they use their free morning or afternoon at the gym, shopping or doing housework. One teacher comes in at lunchtime raring to go after spending the morning on the golf course. The headteacher says that the move has done wonders for staff morale. He justifies it by saying that taxpayers get good value out of the school's teachers who typically spend three days a week running extra-curricular sport, art, music and homework clubs, plus working at weekends and during holidays (Mansell, 2002).

Meetings

Meetings take up a lot of time but they don't have to happen on the school premises. Some people are creative in thinking of venues that make working more enjoyable. How about discussing the school development plan in the jacuzzi at the local health club? Chapter 8 has ideas on managing meetings so that they make best use of people's time.

Training or INSET days are meant to be used for staff training but some schools interpret that notion creatively. The Westborough Primary in Southend, Essex hit the national headlines because they spent one of their training days at Ascot races. The headteacher said the trip had been an important get-together aimed at team-building. She said staff had been owed the time off because of extra hours worked. The Ascot trip was offered to all 129 staff at the school, including catering staff and cleaners. The head added: 'As well as looking after the needs of children, I have to look after staff needs. Sometimes they just need to be together as people. That's crucial and that's why the school is so successful' (BBC, 2003).

Another primary school spent a training day in Amsterdam. The whole school was involved in an art project and so teaching and support staff went to the Rijksmuseum and worked in teams to gather information, ideas and resources, and then plan exciting activities for their year groups. It didn't cost much because the school was near the ferry port. The day was a great success. People bonded and the quality of the creative teaching that the trip inspired resulted in very high quality pupils' work.

Loos

As people who visit many different schools, we are often struck by the poor quality toilet facilities – for both staff and students! There never seem enough loos, especially for women in primary schools. And why does all this matter? We think it matters because, apart from the obvious health and hygiene aspects, it tells us a great deal about how the managers in the school think and care about the staff. We've heard about staff toilets that are permanently locked, and teachers have to ask their head of department for the key. Toilets are an integral part of human life. We pamper ourselves in our bathrooms at home, so why should ones at work invoke so much disdain?

Dame Jean Else, head of Whalley Range high school for girls in Manchester, had the staff toilets painted gold and cream, with stylish fretwork cubicles and potted palms (Leach, 2001). Soft toilet roll, some pot-pourri, a nice handwash dispenser, a towel and hand cream makes such a difference – and it doesn't cost a lot. It's a quick win in terms of improving staff wellbeing and ensuring they feel valued.

Staffrooms

Make sure that you have breaks during the school day – use the staffroom because it can be a great source of support, professionally and socially. But staff working conditions often leave a lot to be desired. Some are dingy, untidy places with poor facilities and mugs that should have health warnings attached. Refurbishing the staffroom is an easy way to make staff feel valued. A dish-washer, a hundred new mugs and glasses, and a machine on the wall that dispenses a never-ending amount of boiling water should, we suggest, be basic. But there needs to be a system for its use. A teacher in a south London second-ary said 'We have had a dishwasher in our staffroom for three years and no one wants either to fill or empty it. The sink is still full of cups' (Craven, 2003).

Schools with cold water dispensers in the staffroom, if not the classrooms, are often calmer places because people aren't wired by caffeine. If there is fruit around, staff will get a boost of energy from snacking on that rather than the usual calorie-laden biscuits.

Some schools have a head of common room/staffroom whose role is to galvanize improvements, ensure that the place is kept tidy and who organises staff events such as trips to the cinema, theatre, etc. They invite outside speakers to talk about the issues the school would like to improve on or ways of helping staff balance their lives, such as through yoga. They set up wellbeing notice boards and a resource library of books, tapes and handouts that staff can use – and contribute to if they wish. Informal social traditions spring up such as the Friday lunchtime or after school drink in the pub. The staff of Ashburton Junior in Croydon have breakfast together on Fridays in the local greasy spoon.

On the other hand at Kemnal Manor secondary school many staff didn't have time to get to the staffroom so it was turned into a classroom that can hold sev-eral classes. Instead there are six satellite areas for staff with facilities such as ICT connections, hot/cold drinks machines and eating areas. Ancillary staff service these satellite areas so that teachers can have food delivered to them if they wish, cups washed, drinks replenished and so on (NRT website, 2004). This sounds like making official the Balkanization (the dominance of departments) that often happens in secondary schools; one wonders what this has done for the whole staff community and communication.

Stukeley Meadows primary school in Huntingdon, Cambridgeshire is part of the Well-Being Programme. Suggestion boxes have sprung up around the school; a termly wellbeing newsletter keeps staff up to date with changes and welcomes new people; there are stress management books in the staffroom and on Fridays the school has relaxation and exercise classes. All support staff, as well as teach-ers, are invited to their once-a-term staff lunch. They are planning a 'pamper yourself' day.

Eating together is a great way to get a group to bond. The staff of St William of York primary school in Lewisham take it in turns to cook a simple lunch for everyone on Fridays. Two parents come in and make the staff lunch on Mondays and Fridays at Tidemill Primary in Lewisham. People get really good healthy food very cheaply and are able to sit down and eat for half an hour rather than having a quick sandwich in the classroom. Other schools pay parents to cook the staff a meal on training days.

Tidemill Primary school staff also make use of an ironing service, which is a helpful timesaver. Staff pay for this, but the school has been able to negotiate a very good rate. They have also organized people to care for teachers' and TAs' children on training days.

Some secondary schools encourage staff to make use of the school's sports facilities – the gym and pool. One special school recognizes the need for staff to keep fit for all the physical work they do with the children.

CONCLUSION

So, there are many things that can be done – indeed are being done – to try to ensure that the school's most important (and expensive!) resource is being looked after. You need to take good care of yourself but we would argue it is an entitlement too. As we noted in Chapter 1, these kind of 'perks' are increasingly becoming the norm and more and more teachers, especially those coming into the profession, are expecting to find them in place. They are useful as aids for recruitment and retention of staff, but we think it is more important than that – schools and the governing bodies that serve them want to be seen as 'good employers', where staff welfare and their training and development are given the priority they deserve. We know for example that nearly 40 per cent of schools are (or are becoming) 'Investors in People' (the government's standard for effective training and development) (Earley and Bubb, 2004). Perhaps this popular kitemark should be extended to cover the kind of issues we've been discussing in this chapter – an *Investor in People and their Wellbeing* perhaps? Now there's an idea!

In the next chapter we look at ways that classroom teachers can make best use of their time – another precious resource!

Section C

Individual and school strategies

Chapter 6

How can teachers save time in the classroom?

> What are the big time-consumers?
>
> Planning
>
> Working with teaching assistants
>
> Marking
>
> Report writing
>
> Display

In Chapter 4 we advocated the use of the ATL self-audit to enable teachers to look carefully and systematically at how they spend their time, whilst the previous chapter looked at ways in which teachers should take good care of themselves. In this chapter the emphasis is on how you can save time by making better use of the limited time at your disposal. We can all work more effectively and knowing how we deploy our most precious resource, time, is the first step on ensuring we 'work smarter rather than harder' – or longer! We begin by considering the main consumers of teachers' time before examining the key areas of planning, working with teaching assistants and support staff, marking, report writing and display. What, then, can be done? How can we approach these areas to help save time and ensure it is spent on things that matter most, such as improving the children's learning experience?

WHAT ARE THE BIG TIME-CONSUMERS?

The 2003 STRB survey of 2,700 randomly selected teachers in primary, secondary and special schools in England and Wales found that on average, primary teachers spend a quarter of their time on preparation and marking. Secondary teachers spend nearly a third of their time on these activities, especially marking pupil work and writing reports. Table 6.1 shows the breakdown of hours and the proportions being spent on different categories of work (for more information see Chapters 1 and 4).

Table 6.1	Average hours worked by classroom teachers (STRB, 2003, Table A5)			
	Average hours		Percentage of total	
	Primary	Secondary	Primary	Secondary
Total	51.8	50.8	100	100
Teaching	18.6	19.6	36	39
Lesson preparation, marking	12.9	14.8	25	29
Non-teaching contact	5.8	6.7	11	13
School/staff managemt	3.9	2.9	8	6
General admin. tasks	6.1	3.6	12	7
Individual/professional	3.2	2.2	6	4
Other activities	1.2	1.1	2	2

PLANNING

Many research projects – our own (Bubb et al., 2003) and others (PriceWaterhouseCoopers, 2001; STRB, 2003) – have found that planning and preparation are significant burdens for teachers. Much of this workload has been driven by the fear that teachers will be called to account by Ofsted inspectors and must have evidence of what has been taught. Local education authority advisers and inspectors can place immense pressure on headteachers to require of teachers detailed planning that is, in fact, unnecessary. Heads themselves can sometimes misinterpret what is expected of schools. Yet Ofsted has insisted that the focus should be on what has been learnt rather than on what has been taught. Its 2000–01 Annual Report states that extensive and overelaborate planning still creates unnecessary pressure on teachers' time.

Planning is an essential aspect of teachers' work but it is time-consuming. All teachers need to plan what they will teach and how they will teach it, but spending excessive amounts of time on long, detailed plans does not necessarily lead to better teaching and learning. Cath Thewlis, headteacher of Pembury School, says, 'You can't knock diligence, but there's a point when diligence starts to sap energy and impact on quality' (NRT website).

Long-term planning

The National Union of Teachers rightly says that it is not reasonable to expect teachers to write new plans for every group or cohort of pupils. Teachers' planning time is reduced in schools where there are well thought through long- and medium-term plans. This should be the case in all but the newest schools and subjects. Every topic that any teacher teaches is likely to have been taught before, so it makes sense to use other people's experience – collaborate, copy and share. Problems arise in places where schemes of work are not in place but the solution is not to devote hours to reinventing the wheel but to contact the LEA, QCA, subject associations and other schools. Time spent finding out what is already out there is time well spent.

Plans can be stored and revised and, often, only minor amendment is necessary. Long- and medium-term plans can be photocopied from the relevant QCA or other curriculum documents, or downloaded from the Internet and then annotated, highlighted and amended.

Primary schools find it hard to cover the overloaded curriculum. Some have found the blocking of foundation subjects to be beneficial. Instead of spending an hour a week on the Romans, for instance, they have a two-day event. This allows children to be more creative, and it's easier to organize additional help and resources. Using curriculum planning software can reduce time and effort. This also makes it easier to reuse planning in future, and make minor modifications.

Fitness for purpose

Plans should be 'fit for purpose'. They should be useful to individual teachers and reflect what they need to be able to teach particular classes. Plans do not have to be very long or complex, but should be kept to a minimum length. They can be set out in the form of bullet points or notes, including how learning objectives will be achieved. Some teachers may want to record more detail than other colleagues – it's a matter of personal choice. Plans are working documents and do not need to be beautifully presented or copied out for others.

With the exception of some children with specific needs, lesson plans for individual pupils are not necessary. There is no prescribed format or length for any teacher's plans. Fitness for purpose is key. All that is specified in the Ofsted framework is that 'teachers plan effectively, using clear objectives that children understand'. Planning should no longer be judged on what's written on paper but on the quality of teaching and learning in lessons that results from it.

The DfES *Time for Standards* (2002a) booklet states that time should be used for aspects of planning that are going to be useful for teachers, and which have a direct impact upon the quality of teaching and learning. People should rarely have to start with a blank sheet when planning for the week ahead.

Using others' plans

Whilst it's true that no plans written by someone else can be completely suitable for an individual teacher or class, taking a pre-prepared plan and adapting it to a particular situation can save you a lot of work – and time. Recycle previously used plans, by annotating them in colour coded pens rather than starting from scratch. The Hamilton Trust posts primary lesson plans on its website (see Appendix) in a campaign to Save Our Sundays! There is a range of high-quality material for all of the primary core and foundation subjects available on the Internet, which many teachers have found to be extremely helpful.

There are many resources available that provide useful starting points and greatly reduce planning time. Good quality plans are already available, such as the National Numeracy Strategy Units and National Literacy Strategy medium-term plans and planning exemplification; and there are ones written by colleagues and many on the Internet. For medium-term planning, the QCA schemes of work contain the detail for each subject. It's not necessary to write things out again. Scribbled Post-its, notes and annotations to add detail that is specific to the class, for example, can easily convert QCA schemes into lesson plans. Planning in this way will meet with Ofsted's approval, providing it has a positive impact on teaching and learning. Planning on the computer saves time substantially in the long term because it's much easier to share plans with colleagues, and also to reuse, copy or adapt them in future. However, handwritten plans may be quicker in the short term.

Teachernet (see Appendix), for example, offers over a thousand lesson plans and resources, which have been evaluated by teachers. These are downloadable in such a way as to enable teachers to alter them to suit their own needs. Links to other relevant materials from reputable sources, such as the QCA and the BBC, are also provided.

Many schools have systems for team planning. Either all the teachers in a primary year group get together to plan everything for the forthcoming week or they divide up the curriculum so that each teacher is responsible for planning a few subjects not only for themselves but for their colleagues too. Sharing will reduce your workload, and you'll get better ideas. Although achievable without it, one major benefit that Brunswick House primary school in Kent has found of giving teachers laptops has been lesson plan and resource sharing. Teachers put their lesson plans and resources on the network, enabling other teachers and TAs to use them.

Kemnal Manor in Bromley has interactive whiteboards (IWBs) in each classroom. The IWBs are connected to the Internet and the teacher's laptop. The teacher prepares all their lessons on their laptop and saves the lessons on a shared drive. This saves teacher time by sharing resources and planning. For example, there are 12 science teachers but each teacher only has to prepare one in 12 lessons as they are all shared. They also introduced a 'virtual learning environment' (VLE) where they put lessons, homework and other resources for the students to access from home. It is planned that parents will be able to access lesson by lesson, live, on-line, attendance data, baseline data and their sons' homework all via the VLE. Parents will be able to see if their son is late for school or late for a lesson in real time!

However, you do need to establish ground rules about fairness and equal contributions. One teacher said, 'I have a head of department who has never produced worksheets or ideas that I could use, but always nicks my stuff'. Her solution is to give her a copy of everything she makes: 'at least that way it's out in the open and she has to thank me for it' (Bubb, 2004b, p. 42).

Resources

Teachers spend a great deal of time making resources and worksheets. Again, think about fitness for purpose. Is it worth spending time on resources in terms of:

- what children will gain from it?

- how long they will use the resource for?

- how many times the resource is going to be used?

- what else you could be doing?

Sometimes professional pride makes teachers do an unnecessarily perfect job. Our advice is to keep things simple. Using ICT to make resources and worksheets will normally save time – and is useful as a way to share and store worksheets so that they can be adapted for future use – but sometimes handwritten versions can be quicker and just as useful. Somebody (in your school or at a neighbouring one) probably has the resources you're looking for, so ask around before you need them. Share resources with teachers of the same year group.

Use or adapt already published worksheets and resources. Organize a system for keeping worksheets and resources so that they can be found the next time they're needed. Use the overhead projector more. If one pupil does their classwork on cheap transparency paper (in black pen so that it can be photocopied for their folder or exercise book) it can be used as an assessment and teaching resource in the plenary and in future lessons.

The Internet can be a great help with finding suitable resources. There are many useful sites (for example, www.physics-online.com; www.theresite.org.uk) that one finds when putting key words into a search engine, such as Google. For instance, physics-online finds the best interactive resources and categorizes them so teachers can get to what they want in seconds. It also provides a straightforward method for combining on-line resources with teachers' own written exercises.

WORKING WITH TEACHING ASSISTANTS

The next chapter is about how support staff can be used across the school but in this chapter we focus on ideas and issues for what they can do in the classroom because there are plans to have 50,000 more support staff in schools by 2006 (DfES, 2003) – most of them providing in-class support in the roles of teaching assistants (TAs) and learning support assistants (LSAs). This means that teachers will have to manage the work of other adults, as well as the learning of the pupils. Most support staff are of high quality, but some can prove challenging to manage. Table 6.2 has some issues identified by teachers, with a few suggestions for solutions.

Table 6.2   **Problems with support assistants (Bubb, 2004a, p. 82)**

Issue	Ideas/solutions
Being unsure of the additional adult's role.	Find out exactly what they are paid to do. For instance, some special needs assistants are funded to work with individual SEN pupils.
Not sure when they are going to be in the class.	Find out exactly when they're coming and make sure they know that you're expecting them.
Not wanting to ask them to do menial tasks.	Again, look at their job description. Most are happy to help out.
Some do too much for the children and encourage over dependence.	Model the sort of teaching you want. Don't be afraid to mention concerns – they haven't benefited from training like yours and so are usually more than pleased to be given advice.
Some have little control over the children.	Again, model how to manage behaviour. Speak to their line manager if it's a big problem.
Some can take over the class.	This is very tricky. Speak to them about the need to establish yourself as the teacher, but otherwise get advice on how to deal with this.
Some talk when the teacher has asked for everyone's attention	Theatrically or humorously emphasize that you need *everyone's* attention.
Some don't do quite what you've asked them to.	Explain, model, write instructions; speak to them about your concern.
Some are stuck in their ways and do not like new ideas and practices.	Tricky. Try to get them on your side by asking for their advice, their patience in trying things out.
Planning for them, but they do not turn up.	Make sure they and others know how much you depend on and value them. Make a fuss if they're taken away too often.

Time to talk

It's very hard for teachers to find time to talk to other adults who are working in the class. This often means that they are not used to best effect because the teacher needs to explain the activity and what they should do. A plan that can be given to them at an appropriate time should help (see Table 6.3). Considering how to allocate TAs' working hours is essential. People who don't start work until after teaching has commenced will not be able to discuss what role they should take. Many schools have rearranged TAs' working hours to allow opportunities to talk to teachers.

Whole-class teaching

Teachers need to think about what they want other adults to do during the whole-class teaching parts of the lesson. This could be a time to prepare resources or for them to be involved with certain children – checking their understanding, for instance. Additional adults will want to know which children to support and where they should work. Most importantly, they need to know what the children should do, what they should do to help them and what the children should learn. Giving the adult a list of resources that they will need means that they can be responsible for getting them out.

Even when the teacher is teaching the whole class, there's a role for the teaching assistant in oiling the discussion by drawing in reticent pupils, starting the ball rolling when they are slow to contribute and joining in. Teaching assistants can help to prevent and manage incipient behaviour problems by:

- sitting alongside a difficult child so they can be settled and involved

- focusing the attention of inattentive pupils on the teacher, by directing them to look, answer or apply themselves to questions as appropriate

- eye contact, by sitting at the front rather than the back, so facial gestures can be seen

- learning support for children who need specific help to access the lesson.

Confident teaching assistants help deliver the lesson. They might echo the teacher by repeating, rewarding or refining teaching points, e.g. repeating or rephrasing instructions for pupils who are slow to respond: 'That's right – look for the speech marks.' The most obvious benefit of teaching assistants is the presence of an extra pair of eyes (and ears) for:

- observing individual pupils

- noting who 'can' and who 'can't'

- picking up emergent issues

- comparing notes and giving feedback to the teacher.

Table 6.3 Plan for an additional adult (Bubb, 2003b, p. 52)

Name: *Lesson and time:*
What to do while I am whole-class teaching: Introduction   Plenary
Pupils to support: Where and when
Activity: What the pupils should do: What I would like you to do: What I want them to get out of it: Things that they will need:
How did they get on?   Thank you!

Additional adults have important information about the children they work with. They often know more about the children with special needs, for instance, than the class teacher. These insights can be tapped by asking the adult to make some notes about how the children got on (see Table 6.3).

MARKING

Marking pupils' work takes a long time for all teachers, but it's worse in certain subjects such as secondary English. Teachers may wish to consider why they mark work. Responses might include any of the following:

- I have to

- Other staff expect it

- Pupils expect it

- Parents expect it

- It's useful

- It gives me a picture of the pupil's understanding and achievement.

Do the rewards, in terms of feedback to pupils that they read and act upon to improve their learning, merit the time spent on marking? One wants to maximize the usefulness of marking, while allowing time to plan, make and gather resources – and have a life. How long are people spending on marking? Ask them to estimate how much marking (of class work and homework) they have to do in a week and at what level, and then ask them to audit what they actually do. Estimate how much marking (of class work and homework) you have to do in a week and at what level. You should keep a record (such as through the audit process in Chapter 4) so that you know the scale of the problem. It's so easy to let marking spread over a longer time than it should.

Different pieces of work require different levels of marking. There will be occasions when a Rolls Royce product is needed but at other times something more everyday is fine. A marking schedule (eg. Y7 Monday, Y9 Tuesday, Y10 Wednesday, Y8 Thursday, Y11 + 10 Weekend) can help people manage what can be a very stressful burden.

Encourage people to discuss how they manage their marking. How long does it take them? When do they do it? What tips do they have? Little things such as collecting books so that they're open at the right page for marking can make a real difference. Do teachers deliberately plan work that doesn't take so long to mark, but which still meets learning objectives? Look at some examples of people's marking but avoid competitiveness – a one-upmanship of rigorous marking will make everyone's life harder. Build a bank of useful marking phrases and questions, instead of the everyday 'Good', to help you. Some teachers swear that stickers and stampers ('Well done, you've met your objective') save time and motivate pupils.

Different sorts of marking

Perhaps teachers could benefit from extending their range, by considering different sorts of marking:

- children 'marking' their own and each other's work

- self-assessment

- pupils mark their work during the plenary

- quick ticking and checking as pupils' work

- using stampers ('good effort', 'excellent!')

- use codes (sp, underline) that pupils understand rather than full sentences

- grading

- selective marking – ignoring all but answers to key questions

- brief comment against the learning intention

- detailed comment against the learning intention

- traffic-light marking – pupils put a green mark against work where they feel they've met the learning objective or a red mark where they haven't understood it. This enables teachers to prioritize those pupils with difficulties.

Are you making the most of all the different sorts of marking? Remember that peer review and self-assessment are very valuable as well as potentially less time-consuming for teachers since they'll be in the role of 'moderator'. Balance out work that needs marking over the week so that you don't have too much at one go. Decide what seems a realistic amount of time to spend on marking and when to get it done to fit in with other commitments. Try to stick to this 'timetable', aiming to reduce the time and to do things earlier and more quickly, if possible.

Lessons with a clear learning intention will enable teachers to write specific assessment criteria – the things that pupils might do towards meeting the learning intention partially or fully. Shirley Clarke (1998) recommends using the acronyms WALT and WILF. WALT (we are learning to ...) is a way of sharing the learning intention with pupils. This can then be refined for different groups of pupils through telling them WILF (what I'm looking for). Teachers can print assessment criteria directly onto worksheets for pupils and teachers to make abbreviated judgements against. These can be differentiated. For instance, in a lesson on fractions with a mixed ability class, a teacher wrote assessment criteria onto the worksheets that she could quickly tick, cross or comment on.

Peer review is a very useful form of marking. Plan some time for pupils to swap books and 'mark' each other's. Ideally do this before the end of the lesson so that they can improve their work before the lesson finishes. This will be truly formative marking. Pupils are rarely silly or rude about each other's work, but pairings will need to be considered carefully. Putting together people who are friends and whose work is of a similar standard works well. Pairing people who speak the same mother tongue can also be advantageous, because they can explain things to each other in their own language. Obviously pupils will copy the marking style that they have experienced, so teachers' one-to-one marking will have countless spin-offs.

Many teachers note points that many pupils had difficulty with on a lesson plan so that it can feed into teaching. Focusing on how well pupils have met the learning objectives is easier said than done, particularly in a piece full of errors. What should teachers do about spelling mistakes, for instance? What about handwriting, grammar and punctuation? When will the pupils have time to read and respond to marking, by correcting and learning spellings, for example?

REPORT WRITING

Reports take ages to write. Don't be deceived by report writing computer programmes – the process still takes ages. Table 6.4 has an action plan that shows how this enormous task can be broken down into manageable chunks. If you're writing reports in a new school, find out what's required: whether there's a computer programme, who will work out the attendance figures, how much detail to write. Some schools opt for something quite minimalist, but others require lengthy paragraphs. Teachers need to fit in with the school style. Ask pupils to do a self-assessment – what they're good at, have enjoyed, need to improve. Their information will help teachers write one or two very personal points that mean that the report gives a flavour of the individual.

Many schools use a computer programme for reporting. All pupils' details are on disc. All a teacher has to do is input comments into the automatically tailored template and cut and paste the comments of other relevant staff. Wombwell High School in Barnsley has introduced computer-generated interim reports four to six times per year. These include information on attendance, behaviour, rewards and sanctions, external and internal exam results and effort grades. The reports are used to support the school's mentoring system – where a pupil and a mentor meet six times a year to discuss progress. These meetings rely on the up-to-date information contained in the report. More than half of the meetings are attended by parents. The database has enabled more focused personal contact with individual pupils. Prior to meetings, the head and the deputy analyse data and talk to heads of department about the 'at risk' areas for individual pupils.

| Table 6.4 | An action plan for writing reports |

Name: Date: Date objective to be met:

Objective: Write annual reports to parents that give a clear picture of children's progress and achievements by 25th June.

Success criteria	Actions	Suggested dates	Actual dates	Progress Notes
You have an evidence base – i.e. you know what each child can do.	Collate assessment information so that you know what each child can do in the key aspects of every subject. Gather information from other teachers if necessary. Fill gaps in knowledge of what class can do. Give pupils a self-assessment so that you have insight into what they think they've learnt and their greatest achievements.	19 April		
You know what the school expects.	Find out the school system for writing reports – speak to the assessment co-ordinator. Read some examples that have been identified as being good. Note stylistic features and key phrases.	26 April		
You have written one report to an acceptable standard.	Read the children's previous year's report. Write one child's report in draft. Give to the head teacher for comment.	21 May		
You have a timetable that will enable you to meet the deadline.	Set up the system for reports (i.e. computer format). Draw up a timetable of when you're going to write the reports, allowing about two hours for first five, one hour for next 20, three-quarters for last five, one-third over half term. Liaise with other teachers who are contributing to the reports.	24 May		
You meet the deadline.	Write the reports. Give them to the headteacher for checking and signing. Celebrate!	22 June		

Managing Teacher Workload © Sara Bubb and Peter Earley 2004

● Report-writing checklist:

● Draw up a timetable of when you're going to write your reports.

● Speak to others about how they go about them.

● Read old reports to get a feel for style and useful phrases.

● Write a straightforward report first.

● Ask the children to do a self-assessment.

● Think of the overall big message.

● Write succinctly and avoid jargon.

● Start with positive comments.

● Phrase negatives positively.

● Suggest what the pupil has to do to improve.

● Get a few checked by a senior member of staff before you do the rest.

Ask yourself:

● Have I commented on all the necessary areas?

● Have I made any spelling or grammatical mistakes?

● Will the parent/carer understand it?

● Does it give a clear, accurate picture?

● Is it positive?

● Are weaknesses mentioned?

DISPLAY

Clean and tidy classrooms create a good atmosphere across the school. When things aren't organized there is a downward cycle: there's more graffiti and litter because there's nothing nice to take pride in. Colourful and bright displays can cheer up the classroom and make it a more pleasant environment, while allowing peripheral learning to occur – if 'because' is looked at enough, surely children will be able to spell it correctly! Displaying pupils' work encourages them to take pride in their work and can motivate them. However, it is time-consuming.

According to the new workload or remodelling programme, teaching assistants should do displays but teachers need to tell them what is wanted in some detail. Getting ideas for displays can be hard, so keep photos of displays, look around the school and in books, and ask others for inspiration. There are always people in school who love display and will be more than happy to help. In fact, many find it a really creative, relaxing and rewarding part of teaching. Here are some tips that teachers have shared, that may be useful to teaching and support staff:

- Word process labels – and keep them on file for the future.

- Laminate labels that can be used again.

- Laminate small labels with pupils' names on for attaching to their work.

- Involve the pupils, e.g. in writing labels, mounting work and finding artefacts.

- Incorporate the making of a display into a lesson.

- Pre-cut paper (to be smaller than A4) for pupils to work on so that it can be mounted on A4 paper and not need trimming.

- Have permanent displays that only need occasional adding to (e.g. literacy – alphabet, key words).

- Attach some card or a coin to your staple gun so that the staple doesn't go all the way in the board but is slightly raised for easy removal. That way work, labels and backing paper won't get torn.

- Save artefacts for displays that you are likely to repeat, such as ones for 'Black History Month'.

CONCLUSION

As with most things, everyone's life is easier if the whole school pulls together. We're all working together, making life easier all round, saving time and working 'smarter not harder'! Not only should working life become more tolerable as the workload is eased, it should also become more enjoyable and professionally satisfying. We know from research into motivation and morale (see, for example, Evans, 1999) that schools where high levels of both are found are those that work together, where collaboration and collegiality are important – they are also schools that are well led and managed and that make good use of all staff, including support staff. In the next chapter we consider the organization and deployment of support staff, while Chapter 8 focuses on the key role of school leaders.

Chapter 7

Support staff: what do we need to think about?

- The range of support staff
- Support staff taking classes
- Higher level teaching assistants
- Administrative support
- Bursars

In the previous chapter we discussed how teachers can work successfully with support staff and outlined some of the main issues that may arise. In this chapter we examine further the role and function of support staff – or paraprofessionals as they are increasingly called – to raise a number of questions about their deployment in schools. Clearly such staff are indispensable to the success of the remodelling programme, but their growth in numbers and widening of role raises some fundamental questions which we suggest may not always have been clearly thought through and which have major implications for the future of the teaching profession.

THE RANGE OF SUPPORT STAFF

Greater flexibility in school budgets and the government's remodelling programme has meant the number and range of support staff working in schools has increased considerably over the last decade, and especially in the last few years. Table 7.1 shows that the total number of support staff rose by 8,300 to reach 225,300 in January 2003; the number of teaching assistants rose by 15,900 to reach 122,300; the number of administrative staff rose by 800 to reach 50,600 (DfES, 2003b). In many schools, support staff outnumber the teaching staff.

Table 7.1	Numbers of support staff (DfES, 2003b, Table 13)

Support staff in maintained nusery, primary, middle and secondary schools, special schools and pupil referral units in England[1]

Full-time equivalents: January of each year

	1997	1998	1999	2000	2001	2002	2003 (p)
Teaching assistants[2]							
Teaching assistants	35.5	38.8	39.3	45.3	55.6	57.3	73.1
Special needs support staff	24.5	26.0	29.5	32.4	37.7	46.7	46.8
Minority ethnic pupil support staff	1.2	1.5	1.5	2.1	2.5	2.5	2.5
Total	61.3	66.3	70.3	79.8	95.8	106.4	122.3
Administrative staff							
Secretaries	27.6	28.5	29.1	30.2	30.6	25.6	24.7
Bursars	4.1	4.2	4.4	4.7	5.0	4.9	5.1
Other admin/clerical staff	7.5	7.3	7.7	8.3	10.7	19.3	20.8
Total	39.2	40.1	41.2	43.2	46.3	49.8	50.6
Technicians							
Total	12.7	13.1	13.5	14.2	15.0	16.6	18.0
Other support staff							
Matrons/nurses/medical staff[3]	1.2	1.2	1.2	1.2	1.2	1.8	1.7
Child care staff (boarding schools)[4]	3.4	3.4	3.1	3.3	3.2	3.2	0.4
Other[5]	18.7	19.7	22.1	23.1	27.4	39.3	32.3
Total	23.3	24.4	26.5	27.5	31.8	44.2	34.4
Total support staff	136.5	143.8	151.5	164.7	189.0	217.0	225.3
(total excluding nursery schools)	134.1	141.5	149.0	162.1	186.3	214.2	222.4

Notes:

(p) provisional

1. Includes non-maintained special (and special and general hospital schools).
2. Includes nursery assistants in nursery schools.
3. Included with 'other' in nursery schools.
4. Due to a reporting problem at source, the number of child care staff has not been recorded accurately by schools, resulting in child care staff being distributed across other support staff categories.
5. Includes: librarians, welfare assistants, learning mentors and any other support staff regularly employed in schools; matrons, nurses, other medical staff in nursery schools.

There are not only greater numbers of support staff, but the range of their roles has increased. The DfES distinguishes between five broad types of support staff:

- pedagogical

- behaviour and guidance

- administration and organization

- pedagogic/technical

- administration and organization/environment and catering.

Table 7.2 illustrates the sorts of support staff that might be included under each category. However, one of the problems with such lists is that schools have a confusing array of different terms for people who do very similar jobs. Acronyms abound: people who help children in class are known as TAs, HLTAs, LSAs, TPAs, WAs, SNAs, LRAs, LMs and helpers. Roughly translated, this means teaching assistants, higher level teaching assistants, learning support assistants, teachers' personal assistants, welfare assistants, special needs assistants, learning resource assistants, learning mentors and helpers. The list of abbreviations at the front of this book will come in handy! Much of the difference in title has to do with traditions, on the one hand (the name stays the same but the role has changed), and an attempt to recognize that jobs have changed, on the other hand. Status is a key factor in deciding which titles are used, and this is important because support staff have traditionally had low status in schools.

Table 7.2	Types of support staff (based on Johnson et al. 2004)	
Pedagogical	*Behaviour and Guidance*	*Administration and organization*
Teaching assistants	Connexions personnel advisers	Bursars/business managers
Higher level teaching assistants	Counsellors	Financial technician
Nursery nurses	Learning mentors	School secretary
Music specialists	Midday supervisors	Administrative office staff
Language assistants	Education welfare officers	Receptionist
Bilingual support assistants	Youth workers	School nurse
Library/information assistants		
Playworkers		
Sports coaches		
Pedagogic/technical		*Administration and organization/environment and catering*
DT technicians		Premises managers/caretakers
ICT/technical support staff		Cleaners/premises staff
Science technicians		Catering/kitchen manager
		Catering/kitchen staff

One thing that schools will need to think about carefully is what titles fit job descriptions best. In this rapidly changing field where support staff are having to change more than teachers, clear job descriptions are fundamental to the success of remodelling. For instance, Barbara Redhead, the headteacher of Wyndham primary school in Newcastle, has rewritten job descriptions to merge lunchtime and classroom assistant work (Redhead, 2004). But another problem with trying to classify or label support staff is that in practice individual people might have several roles within a day. For instance, many teaching assistants, who do everything from the photocopying and washing paint pots to taking the whole class, may also be midday supervisors and first aiders.

A long-serving teaching assistant working with Year 7 pupils explains all of the additional functions she now performs in addition to being the named person for Social Services and co-ordinating First Aid:

> *I now do CAT tests, accelerated reading, paired reading, IEP completion and annual reviews of pupils, because I see them across the curriculum. I handle school problems and have greater relationships with the Year 7 parents. I deal with induction of new staff, whole-class support preparing worksheets, ICT programmes and differentiation for different pupils.*

(NRT website)

Let's look at the new support staff that one school has employed as a result of remodelling the workforce. Penketh High, a 1,400-pupil secondary school in Warrington has 80 teachers and 60 support staff. Its new support staff include:

- eight learning resource administrators (LRAs), each assigned to a department area

- six SEN teaching assistants

- three learning mentors

- a team of exam invigilators, organized by an 'exam consultant'

- a business manager

- a 'consultant' to support arts provision and the school's specialist school (visual and media) bid

- a consultant (ex-teacher) who organizes work experience visits

- seven technicians – three for science, one for food, one for design, one for ICT and one jointly appointed primary/secondary ICT technician /LRA

- a dedicated reprographics department manager plus a part-time assistant

- a professional development manager

- a community development manager charged with providing activities, mainly sport and recreation, in the evening and holidays for the community

- a library manager.

Look at the titles people have: library manager, reprographics department manager, exam consultant and learning resource administrators. All sound very high status.

But how is all this paid for? Barry Fishwick, the headteacher says:

> *This constitutes a substantial investment. It's all been paid for from our existing budget. We've had to be very creative. The percentage of budget given to staffing has increased in line with the increase in staff. Other money has also been invested. For example, the school used all of its 'Inclusion' funding to pay for new TAs.*

(NRT website)

SUPPORT STAFF TAKING CLASSES

The government specifies teaching work as:

- planning and preparing lessons and courses for pupils

- delivering lessons to pupils

- assessing the development, progress and attainment of pupils

- reporting on the development, progress and attainment of pupils, and

- marking the work of pupils.

These duties are carried out by teachers on a day-to-day basis but, if schools so choose, they can be carried out by a range of support staff, subject to a system of supervision. For example, there are activities that support learning such as finding, selecting and co-ordinating resources, which do not necessarily need to be done by a qualified teacher.

But perhaps asking support staff to do tasks traditionally done by teachers is just shifting the burdens of stress and long working hours to others. Although the NRT website is full of quotations from support staff saying how rewarding their new responsibilities are and how their status has been considerably enhanced, is this the whole picture? Will teaching assistants feel unduly stressed about taking a whole class?

Pupils must not suffer from the remodelling of the school workforce – they should benefit. But how does the principle of support staff teaching classes marry with the raising standards agenda? One might suppose that children will make less progress with a teaching assistant taking them than with their teacher, and if this is to happen half a day a week so that their teachers can plan and prepare, will standards suffer? What about managing behaviour? Newly qualified and supply teachers get a rough ride from pupils. Surely the same will be true of teaching assistants and cover supervisors?

Remodelling has by and large been good for teachers but teaching assistants taking classes is a real sticking point. Gerald Haigh (2004) writing for the *TES* calls it 'the classic encounter between the irresistible force and the immovable object' – the pragmatists and the principled.

It's not difficult to see the argument for being able to put a teaching assistant in charge of a class. It is convenient to be able to use TAs to achieve flexibility of organization – freeing an induction tutor to do a lesson observation on an NQT for example. Financially, schools would make a great saving. The cost-effectiveness of external supply teachers is an issue. For instance, Easington school, a 980-pupil secondary in Durham, spent £203,194 on supply cover in 2002–03 and didn't always feel they had value for money. For covering short-term absence, a TA who knows the school, the children and the systems might be better than taking pot luck with a supply teacher who may not have the required knowledge. At Haberdashers Aske's in Lewisham, technicians are used to teach specific ICT skills to some students at Key Stage 3 and to supervise classes when teachers are absent.

Many schools now have 'cover supervisors'. Kemnal Technology College in Bromley has 5.4 full-time equivalent cover supervisors: 'They have a laptop, plug it in to our shared drive and download an appropriate pre-prepared cover lesson. This ensures that when a teacher is absent the students do not miss out. We are now a no teacher cover school and staff attendance has improved' (NRT website). Easy! Or is it? And is it right? Here's where the principles come in, shouting above the pragmatics. As a profession, we've worked over the years to ensure that we have an all-graduate teaching force, and to raise the status of teaching as a profession. How does this marry with letting a teaching assistant take the class? Perhaps schools don't need qualified teachers at all, if it's so easy. There's a feeling that although the workload agreement says that teachers and support staff are not interchangeable, maybe what is really going on is an erosion of the profession and the making of cheaper education.

Keeping class sizes down to below 30 has also been an aim of many heads and teachers. However, Kemnal Manor in Bromley – one of the 32 pathfinder schools – has a strategy of teaching large classes at times. For instance, one maths teacher teaches large groups of students supported by three classroom assistants. The teacher connects a laptop with the teaching materials into two connected interactive whiteboards and there is a radio microphone so that all students can hear. The teacher prepares the lessons, gives the introduction, helps during the lesson and gives the plenary at the end. The classroom assistants call the register, give out any equipment and do all the marking.

So, will the increase in support staff mean fewer jobs for teachers? The Secondary Heads Association (SHA) and the National Association of Schoolmasters/Union of Women Teachers (NASUWT) both think the transfer of administrative tasks to support staff could eventually, in some schools, lead to an overall reduction in teaching posts. John Dunford, SHA general secretary, said that transferring administrative tasks to support staff would leave teachers with more teaching time and so fewer of them would be needed. The overall reduction in the teacher workforce would be slight and would happen over time through natural wastage. Chris Keates, NASUWT deputy general secretary, said 'You might have needed three teachers previously whereas now you may need 2.4 teachers because there are fewer administrative tasks' (Stewart, 2004). The biggest teaching union remains outside the remodelling agreement. The National Union of Teachers (NUT) remains convinced that the workload deal damages the professional interests of teachers.

Pay

Support staff are largely made up of local parents, usually mothers, for whom working in their children's school has enormous benefits. They are thus easy to exploit, but is that any reason to do so? A delegate at the Association of Teachers and Lecturers' 2004 annual conference in Bournemouth accosted Stephen Twigg, the Minister for Schools (Parkinson, 2004). Why, he asked the Minister in front of an assembled press corps, was his wife paid less than a Tesco checkout assistant? Marion Bevan, who went to school with Stephen Twigg and who has a degree in social science and a postgraduate certificate in child development, takes home £5.70 an hour for her work with children at Chalkwell Hall Infant School in Southend.

Teaching assistants at Pembury primary school in Kent are already paid at a higher rate than most of their colleagues in other schools, as the headteacher reviewed their pay scales a couple of years before the remodelling process. The TAs receive an additional honorarium for cover supervisory work, which they can take either as money or as time in lieu.

So some TAs get paid more (though not much more), but there is no nationally agreed pay scale for support staff unless people are put on the unqualified teacher pay scales, which at present (summer 2004) range from £14,490 to £22,395 a year. Many local authorities are now reviewing support staff pay in the light of the agreement – commonly known as the Single Status Agreement – made in 1997 by the National Joint Council for Local Government Services. In October 2003 the NJC issued guidance called *School Support Staff – the Way Forward* (NJC, 2003) on the employment of school support staff, including examples of job profiles that can be used to support job evaluations and advice on training and development. Until there is at least a local grading and pay structure – if not a national one – in place, there will be great anomalies and possible exploitation.

Support staff contracts vary too. Many are only paid by the hour and only for the time worked during the term, not for holidays. Penketh High found support staff contracts far more complicated and time-consuming than teachers to manage, so they rationalized them so that people either work half a week or a full week.

Finding good support staff

Are schools in certain areas going to have access to a smaller and less qualified or dedicated pool of potential support staff? The demographics of the school's locality are likely to affect the number and type of person in this pool of labour. In many areas, both parents have to work in jobs that pay a decent wage. The quality of support staff is fantastic in some schools but others find it difficult to get the right sort of people – and there's a limit to how much training can be given. Retention of support staff may become a problem as pay and contracts improve in some schools at a faster rate than others, and as teaching assistants leave to train as teachers. Mark Elms headteacher of Tidemill Primary in Lewisham is very concerned with the status of TAs:

We need to consider on- and off-site training and qualifications, accreditation for previous experience, job descriptions and pay. We need to map out the range and diversity of the roles and responsibilities our TAs have and implement a hierarchy of job descriptions that recognises the various levels. Basically, we need to put into place a career structure.

(NRT website)

Form tutors

Some of the learning support assistants at Ninestiles School, Birmingham have taken on the role of form tutor, as a way to create smaller tutor groups thus allowing an enhanced monitoring role for the job of the form tutor in general. The pastoral deputy headteacher believes that this benefits pupils because 'the LSAs meet the emotional needs of the pupils in ways that some overloaded teachers would be stretched to achieve'. He also feels that the tutorial role provides a tremendous boost to the status and esteem of LSAs in the eyes of both pupils and teachers.

The LSA form tutors have networked laptops. They quickly became proficient in dealing with email, especially to communicate with subject staff about pupils in their form groups. Issues around illness, minor learning or behaviour problems could be dealt with quickly, leaving quality face-to-face time for more serious matters. The headteacher has enrolled some of them on counselling courses (NRT website).

Training

Nobody wants TAs to revert to their old paintbrush-cleaning role but they need good training and support. There are now nationally recognized qualifications developed specifically for teaching assistants, which provide clear progression routes into and within employment. The DfES has provided materials encouraging TAs to take part in accredited courses. For those TAs interested in their own professional development and who wish to progress, a co-ordinated and accredited programme of national vocational qualifications (NVQs) and vocationally relevant qualifications (VRQs) was approved in 2001. The Local Government National Training organization has developed a suite of national occupational standards for TAs, which include NVQs at levels 2 and 3. There are two NVQs specifically developed for teaching assistants on the national qualifications framework – one at level 2 (suitable for people new to the role or whose responsibilities at work are limited in scope) and one at level 3 (suitable for experienced teaching assistants whose working role calls for competence across a varied range of responsibilities).

There are also specialist courses available to classroom assistants to work towards qualified teacher status. Teaching assistants who have successfully completed a specialist teacher assistant (STA) course can use these for credit towards a higher level qualification. There are also foundation degrees specifically for teaching assistants.

The DfES has produced lots of support materials for teaching assistants and provides a regional induction programme, which they plan to extend to all support staff (DfES, 2002a). There is an induction training file for newly-appointed assistants and a 'good practice guide' for their management (DfEE, 2000a; 2000b). New TAs are provided with four days of training, to which their mentor must accompany them for one and half days. The teaching assistant induction materials include modules such as:

- How Children Learn (Primary)
- ICT (Primary)
- Role and Context (Primary/Secondary)
- Inclusion, SEN and Disabilities (Secondary)
- Supporting in Secondary Science.

The DfES have developed two videos called *Working with Teaching Assistants in Primary Schools* (DfES/0114/2003) and *Working with Teaching Assistants in Secondary Schools* (DfES/0115/2003). Both are available to order by calling the DfES publication line on 0845 60 222 60. The purpose of the videos is to show how a variety of schools around the country have raised the profile, and developed the role and responsibilities, of their TAs.

HIGHER LEVEL TEACHING ASSISTANTS

For the very best TAs there is now a new status to which they can aspire – to be a higher level teaching assistant (HLTA). The HLTA is a status based on an individual's capacity to meet nationally agreed standards of professionalism, knowledge and skills; it is not a qualification and, significantly, it isn't linked to extra pay. It doesn't replace the NVQs or STA qualifications but nor does it require people to have done those sorts of courses. Having HLTA status doesn't automatically mean that an individual is employed in that capacity. The Education Act 2002 (section 133) sets out the regulatory framework in which HLTAs can be deployed: headteachers are responsible for whom they employ and how they are deployed. However, there is strong emphasis that the work of an HLTA is carried out under the direction of a teacher with regard to providing due notice, preparation and planning, supervision and guidance.

Following consultation, the DfES and the TTA published national standards for HLTAs in September 2003 (TTA, 2003). These are organized in three sections:

1   Professional values and practice. These standards set out the attitudes and commitment expected from those who achieve HLTA status. They aren't a doddle though. For instance, for standard 1.1 they have to 'have high expectations of all pupils; respect their social, cultural, linguistic, religious and ethnic backgrounds; and are committed to raising their educational achievement'.

2   Knowledge and understanding. Those meeting the HLTA Standards must demonstrate sufficient knowledge and understanding to be able to help the pupils they work with make progress with their learning. This knowledge and understanding will relate to a specialist area which could be subject-based or linked to a specific role (e.g. in support of an age phase or pupils with particular needs). These standards cover knowledge of the school curriculum, the expectations required of pupils, the main teaching methods and the testing/examination frameworks in the subjects and age ranges in which they are involved. Here is an example:

    '2.3 They understand the aims, content, teaching strategies and intended outcomes for the lessons in which they are involved, and understand the place of these in the related teaching programme.'

3   Teaching and learning activities. These standards require support staff to demonstrate that they can work effectively with individual pupils, small groups and in whole class settings under the direction and supervision of a qualified teacher. They also require them to demonstrate that they can contribute to a range of teaching and learning activities and to demonstrate skills in planning, monitoring, assessment and class management. Here is an example:

    '3.3.5 They advance pupils' learning in a range of classroom settings, including working with individuals, small groups and whole classes where the assigned teacher is not present.'

As you can see these are not easy and those of you familiar with the standards for qualified teacher status may notice some alarming similarities. The handbook of guidance explains the standards further and has real-life examples of the types of evidence people have used.

There are two routes to HLTA status:

- assessment-only – for support staff who are already at or near the standards to achieve HLTA status swiftly

- full training – designed for people who require training to meet the standards. There are 20 days of training delivered in a centre away from the support staff member's school, but supported by school-based activities and an element of e-support.

During 2004–05, funding from the TTA will be available to train approximately 7,000 people, rising to around 14,000 in 2005–06 and reaching 20,000 by 2006–07.

ADMINISTRATIVE SUPPORT

Photocopying, invariably an irksome chore in most schools, has been decentralized at Wombwell High (NRT website, 2004). To cut the amount of time teachers spent on routine admin tasks, Wombwell High recruited a team of department assistants, working one full or two half days per week in each department. The assistants are aligned to specific departments so teachers can go directly to them rather than through another level of bureaucracy. They take on tasks such as putting up displays, general organizing, photocopying, typing and filing. An administration manager oversees their work, co-ordinating their training and looking out for upcoming administration-heavy events.

Some schools have a job board or box in the staffroom. Teachers identify tasks that need doing, and post them on the board. Teaching assistant teams go to the board and select a task to carry out.

Hartsdown Technology College reviewed the arrangements for collecting cash from students in registration periods for school visits, school fund and charity collections. As a result all cash collection has been transferred to the school office with significant saving in scarce tutorial time, estimated at 315 hours per year.

However, as we said earlier in this chapter, perhaps asking support staff to do tasks traditionally done by teachers is just shifting the burdens of stress and long working hours to others. A secondary school secretary complains,

Previously, I was a bog-standard school secretary doing general reception work, answering the phone and getting visitors to sign the book. But in the last couple of months, I have been expected to take on the coordination of staff cover. On some days, I have less than half an hour before lessons begin to rejig the timetable to make sure all classes have adequate cover, including contacting supply agencies. This used to be the job of a senior teacher. She may now do ten hours less a week, but I do ten hours more, and so far no one has offered me extra money.

(Lepowska, 2004b)

Another vision of the frustrations in the real world can be seen in the words of a member of school office staff who posted this on the *TES* on-line staffroom:

> *Had a week already of faffing about with a heap of new tasks, while any hope of completing the budget and more pressing jobs has gone right out the window. I don't feel in control any more. Our school is losing one full-time teacher and one TA due to lack of funds while £25k sits unwanted in a pot for Formula Capital projects.*

(TES website)

BURSARS

This last comment leads us into thinking about how bursars and business managers can play a significant part in school management, bringing their expertise to bear on the planning and management of resources, as well as taking some of the management load off headteachers. Recent research has found that in addition to financial duties, management and leadership roles are increasing in importance. The DfES sees bursars as playing a key role in helping to implement the government's remodelling agenda (DfES, 2002c). Bursars are taking on more diverse functions and needing greater degrees of support and training. The title of 'bursar' is used here broadly, for convenience. But it doesn't matter what name bursars go by – 'school business manager' and 'senior administrative officer' are commonly used alternatives. What matters is that schools secure the managerial, financial, administrative, and other advice and support that a skilled and competent individual can bring.

The DfES's guidance document about bursars is intended to assist heads, governors, and others involved in running schools, who may be thinking of taking on a bursar or developing the contribution of someone already employed by the school. It considers bursar tasks and responsibilities at three levels: 'basic', 'intermediate' and 'advanced'. These descriptors are used to help explain the potential span and range of the role of bursars (DfES, 2002c).

Bursar training leading to a Certificate of School Business Management (CSBM) is available from the National College for School Leadership. This training covers the functions associated with the bursar. It helps participants to:

- manage resources more efficiently, effectively and sensitively

- enhance and renew their understanding of administration and management

- evaluate the efficiency and effectiveness of educational institutions

- evaluate and analyse management strategies that support effective curriculum and learning development

- develop management decision-making skills

- understand the nature of effective schooling in the twenty-first century

- understand the environment within which education is delivered.

The emphasis is on enabling participants to make a greater practical input to schools. As with other NCSL programmes it makes use of a combination of face-to-face and on-line learning. The course is made up of seven modules:

1   The Educational Enterprise

2   Financial Management

3   Human Resource Management

4   Information and Communication Technology, Management Information Systems

5   Facilities Management

6   Risk Management

7   Administrative and Support Services Management.

The CSBM has been accredited by the Institute of Administrative Management (IAM) leading to the award of the 'International Diploma in Administrative Management'. There is also an on-line community of bursars. This network allows people to get information and advice from colleagues in similar circumstances when faced with a particular problem. For more information see the NCSL website at http://www.ncsl.org.uk/bursar or email bursar@ncsl.org.uk.

The type of job done by a bursar depends largely on the needs and circumstances of individual schools. For headteachers or governors the most important thing is to decide what role the bursar should be playing, and how best they can contribute to the smooth running of the school. They have the capability to make a real difference to the workload of headteachers. They can do this directly, taking over many of the detailed administrative tasks which headteachers too often do themselves, as well as some of the leadership functions which are shared by other staff. This is illustrated in the two case examples from Campion secondary school and Hampstead Parochial primary.

Campion School

Campion School in Northamptonshire already had a bursar employed in the tradi-
tional capacity. However, after noting that the bursar had experience of bidding
successfully for major projects at his previous school and following discussions with
the governing body and the head, it was decided to propose a major change in managing the school finances. The then-bursar was appointed as Business Manager, with
time to dedicate to searching out and preparing bids to secure additional project-
related funding, and a new post of financial bursar was created.

Hampstead Parochial School

Hampstead Parochial School in inner London has a secretary and a bursar. The secretary answers the telephone and the front gate to parents and visitors, deals with the
post, carries out all the correspondence for staff, keeping and tracking registers,
inputting attendance data, producing attendance returns, taking messages, and
deals with trip and lunch money collection. Karen Rees describes her responsibilities
as Bursar and Senior Administration Officer:

> I currently manage all the day-to-day tasks of budget management (electronic
> purchase ordering, delivery advice, payment of invoices etc.) and monthly recon-
> ciliation, quarterly returns, ensuring accounts are prepared to audit level and end
> of year reconciliation and reports. I prepare the budget for consideration by the
> headteacher and governors and make any necessary adjustments.
>
> I prepare reports twice termly on the state of the budget for the headteacher and
> governors and attend meetings to answer questions and implement updates. I
> liaise with the headteacher on a weekly basis to discuss budget adjustments
> regarding staffing, the school development plan and building work implications
> and impacts on our budget. I carry out all data administrative tasks, inputting
> data on to an integrated database holding all the information for each pupil in
> the school and completing LEA and DfES returns. I am also responsible for admis-
> sions, personnel matters, staff support and training in ICT, stock and inventory
> control, governor support, health and safety, office management, and liaising
> with parents, staff and suppliers. I am also the Network Support Administrator
> for both networks in the school and sort out many ICT operational problems.

There is no 'one size fits all' bursar – smaller schools sometimes club together to
employ a 'shared bursar' who works with a number of schools and facilitates the
spread of good practice for mutual benefit. There is, for instance, a lead business
manager of the shared School Business Manager (SBM) programme in North

Bristol. The programme involves three SBMs covering eight primary schools, which had no previous bursarial support. Each SBM specializes in different aspects of school management, such as Health and Safety, human resources, and facilities (NRT website).

CONCLUSION

Clearly the role and function of support staff is going to be high on the educational agenda over the next few years. As we noted earlier, the professional associations and not only the NUT – which it will be recalled was not a signatory to the 'historic' agreement signed in January 2003 – are keeping a careful eye on developments both in terms of adequacy of funding to support the agreement, but also the implications for the status of the teaching profession. Also, as we flagged up earlier, what are the implications of these developments for the quality of the pupils' learning experience? The DfES has recently funded a project investigating the role of support staff in the raising of pupil standards, and it will be very interesting to see their main findings. School leaders and managers will have a crucial role to play in this as they do with regard to the whole matter of staff wellbeing and workload. In the final chapter we consider the workload of school leaders and what skills they need.

Chapter 8

How do school leaders develop skills and manage workload?

- Current picture
- Effective leadership and management
- What can be done?
- Conclusion

In this final chapter we give attention to the skills development and workload of school leaders – middle and senior managers – and consider ways in which their wellbeing and workload can be tackled positively. We begin by examining the extent of their workload and how they are currently spending the bulk of their time. The importance of effective leadership and management goes without saying but it is worth briefly reminding ourselves what this looks like within the context of staff workload and wellbeing. The next section deals with this and argues that school leaders have a duty to their schools and to themselves to ensure that the way they lead and manage has positive effects on staff and pupil morale – the two are interrelated – and, ultimately, on pupil learning outcomes. Attending to staff wellbeing, motivation and morale, and workload are, we argue, key functions of the leadership of schools. If these 'human resource' matters are not being addressed the school will not be operating as effectively as it might. Leaders' and managers' skills must therefore be developed to reflect these priorities.

Yet is it the case that school leaders, especially headteachers, often put the needs of others before themselves? Perhaps the government's remodelling programme has increased heads' workloads as they try to protect their staff from additional responsibilities and ensure that teachers' and other staffs' work-life balance is appropriate. School leaders need to be aware of their own situation and it is all too easy to become so concerned about the staff that they ignore their own performance and wellbeing – yet if leaders are overstressed, they are unlikely to be able to support others. The Teacher Support Network (TSN) identifies the common causes of organizational stress as:

- heavy workload

- lack of control over the work

- long working hours

- rapid change with accompanying insecurity and uncertainty

- poor delegation

- poor communication

- distrust of management.

Whatever the case, it is incontrovertible that successful schools with high-performing staff are more likely to be found in schools where the quality of its leadership is high and effective work practices are modelled.

CURRENT PICTURE

Research has shown that the activity called management, whether it be in schools or non-educational sectors, is characterized by a fragmentation of tasks and a myriad of activities, each one usually taking up a relatively short period of time. As one of our deputy head respondents in the ATL project noted, 'My job is a series of spinning plates on poles and the only way to perhaps reduce them is to drop one. The way that is decided is what are the repercussions of dropping a particular plate as opposed to another one' (Bubb et al., 2003, p. 9).

How school managers and leaders 'spin plates' is shown in Tables 8.1, 8.2 and 8.3, which have been taken from the most recent study by the School Teachers' Review Body. The amount of time devoted to different activities by headteachers is shown in Table 8.1, for deputy and assistant heads in Table 8.2 and for heads of department in Table 8.3. Table 8.1 shows that headteachers work, on average, between 55 and 61 hours each week during term time, with secondary heads spending slightly more time on the job than their primary counterparts. A breakdown of their activities show that heads spend some time teaching – nearly five hours per week in primary (where there is a strong likelihood in small schools that the head will be teaching full time) – and two and half hours per week in secondary schools. Secondary school headteachers spend almost eight hours more per week on 'management' than primary heads although, interestingly for both, management activity consumes about one-half of their total time. For deputy and assistant heads the difference between primary and secondary schools is over four hours.

Table 8.1 **Average hours worked by full-time heads (STRB, 2003)**

| | Average hours | | Percentage of total | |
	Primary	Secondary	Primary	Secondary
All	55.5	60.9	100	100
On grouped activities				
Teaching	4.9	2.5	9	4
Lesson preparation, marking	2.9	2.5	5	4
Non-teaching contact	7.9	9.5	14	16
School/staff management	27.7	35.5	50	58
General admin. tasks	5.1	3.4	9	6
Individual/professional	4.8	6.0	9	10
Other activities	2.2	1.5	4	2

Table 8.2 **Average hours worked by full-time deputy and assistant headteachers (STRB, 2003)**

| | Average hours | | Percentage of total | |
	Primary	Secondary	Primary	Secondary
Total	56.4	56.5	100	100
On grouped activities				
Teaching	15.9	10.8	28	19
Lesson preparation, marking	10.8	9.1	19	16
Non-teaching contact	6.5	9.8	12	17
School/staff management	11.1	16.5	20	29
General admin. tasks	5.7	4.4	10	8
Individual/professional	5.3	4.3	9	8
Other activities	1.2	1.6	2	3

Table 8.3 **Distribution of total hours worked by full-time heads of department in secondary schools (STRB, 2003)**

	Average hours	Percentage of total
Total	52.7	100
On grouped activities		
Teaching	18.1	34
Lesson preparation, marking	12.5	24
Non-teaching contact	7.2	14
School/staff management	6.0	11
General admin. tasks	4.7	9
Individual/professional	2.7	5
Other activities	1.6	3

Secondary headteachers spend the least amount of time on general administration but at 3.4 hours that is still 6 per cent of their time. Other school leaders use up 10 per cent of their time on such tasks that could probably be delegated to bursars and administrators as we outlined in the previous chapter. The distribution of total hours worked by full-time heads of department in secondary schools is shown in Table 8.4. On average they were found to work between 50 to 55 hours per week in term time but you can see that 12.5 per cent worked more than 65 hours. In our research on the worktime audit for the ATL we found many leaders feeling overworked and powerless to change:

I am working too long and, therefore, becoming more inefficient. I get few things done to the standard I would like to achieve. I am forever compromising on quality or half completing tasks. This is not professionally rewarding

(Bubb et al., 2003, p. 10).

Table 8.4	Average hours worked by full-time heads of department in secondary schools (STRB, 2003)
Total hours worked	*Percentage of teachers*
Up to 35	3.8
Over 35 up to 40	4.5
Over 40 up to 45	13.5
Over 45 up to 50	18.7
Over 50 up to 55	23.4
Over 55 up to 60	13.1
Over 60 up to 65	10.4
Over 65 up to 70	7.1
Over 70	5.4

As we noted in Chapter 2, under the government's remodelling programme, since September 2003 leadership and management time should have been introduced for teachers with management responsibilities and there are plans, from September 2005, to introduce dedicated leadership time for headteachers. However important this dedicated time is, it could be argued that what matters more is how this time is spent. Is leadership and management time used effectively? Those teachers who have worked in schools where the leadership and management have left a lot to be desired will vouch for its importance and be aware of its crucial role in raising staff motivation and morale, and in managing workload and wellbeing. What then do we know about effective leadership and management and why is it so important?

EFFECTIVE LEADERSHIP AND MANAGEMENT

The literature on school leadership and management has grown rapidly over the last decade or so and reflects the growing interest shown by government (and its agencies) in leaders and their role in school improvement (e.g., see Earley and Weindling, 2004). The National College for School Leadership, set up in November 2000, is the embodiment of that burgeoning interest in leadership and the crucial part it is believed to play in ensuring school success. In 2004 the NCSL distributed to every school in England a pamphlet entitled 'What we know about successful school leadership' (Leithwood and Riehl, 2003). The Canadian authors proposed a core set of leadership practices that they claim form the 'basics' of successful leadership in almost all settings or contexts and organizations. These are outlined under three headings:

- setting directions

- developing people

- developing the organization.

Effective leaders and managers work with and through other people, amongst other things, by providing appropriate models and setting examples for staff and others to follow that are consistent with the school's values and goals. Key activities they undertake include strengthening school culture, modifying organizational structures and developing collaborative processes (Leithwood and Riehl, 2003, pp. 6–7).

More specifically, in relation to workload and wellbeing we have some evidence as to what successful practice looks like. In 2004 Ofsted published a report about the effective leadership and management of the workforce (Ofsted, 2004). It says that schools that manage their workforce effectively to help raise standards are those that actively:

- *manage the culture* by creating a climate in which staff can work together productively

- *manage the staff* by implementing effective policies and procedures which ensure that highly competent people are recruited, deployed, and trained and developed further

- *manage the working environment* by investing in it to make it a place where staff and pupils feel able to work hard and are motivated to do so

- *manage change* by harnessing the energies of the workforce to plan for and introduce changes that lead to better teaching and higher standards.

These are elaborated on in Figure 8.1.

Figure 8.1	Leadership and management: managing the workforce

1. School leaders *managed their cultures* effectively in four ways:
- Managers took deliberate steps to create a culture of openness that embraced all staff, where there was an accessible head, a collaborative ethos, negotiation and consultation about policy decisions, consensus (as far as possible), and a willingness to confront issues and take hard decisions when necessary.
- Schools had a clear set of values and aspirations that the workforce knew and agreed with. Where staff had helped shape them, they generally felt more committed to them.
- Managers recognized the achievements and contributions of staff, individually and in teams, formally and informally. They understood that a workforce that felt valued was likely to be motivated and achieve more highly and encouraged and supported staff to undertake professional development activities.
- Teams were established in which all members of the workforce worked together productively and an inclusive ethos was promoted. Teaching assistants particularly appreciated being recognized as important members of the teaching team.

2. School leaders *managed their staff* effectively in six ways:
- The appointment process was fair and transparent, allowed for some negotiation of roles and responsibilities, and ensured that the most suitable people were appointed to the right jobs and renumerated accordingly. Good succession planning was helped by effective staffing policies and well-devised staff induction arrangements.
- Roles and responsibilities were clearly defined and most staff had clear job descriptions.
- The management and renumeration structures were clear and rational, and informed decisions on pay and staffing.
- Managers deployed teaching and non-teaching staff effectively, and knew how to use and build on their individual strengths. Several schools had recently increased significantly the number of non-teaching staff to carry out the tasks that would otherwise be done by teachers, such as the organization of supply cover, the administration of examinations and management of the learning resources centre.
- Staff were well supported by the school's arrangements for continuing professional development.
- The performance management procedures were used well to support staff development.

3. School leaders *managed the work environment* effectively in three ways:
- The physical environment was improved, where necessary, to provide pleasant working conditions.
- There were successful behaviour management policies and leadership teams were prominent in implementing them.
- Managers were aware of the need to promote a healthy work/life balance and made conscious efforts to help staff manage their workload.

4. School leaders *managed change* effectively in three ways:
- Change, including goverment initiatives, was introduced successfully, because managers saw the potential benefits to the school, presented them to staff in a positive light, and took care to stage and time the introduction of the changes. These changes have generally had a positive effect on the deployment, motivation, development and performance of teachers.
- Information and communication technology (ICT) was used increasingly to support effective management and teaching, and funding was used well to improve ICT resources and develop the skills of staff in their use.
- Managers monitored the effect of their decisions on the work of the school through self-evaluation and external review, and took account of the findings in future planning.

Source: adapted from Ofsted, 2004.

All the areas discussed by Ofsted (2004) and outlined in Figure 8.1 are central features of effective leadership and management and therefore of importance but the third area – *managing the work environment* – is of particular relevance to this chapter. Ofsted notes how effective school leaders tried to promote a healthy work-life balance and made conscious efforts to help staff manage their workload. They state:

> *The more effective senior managers monitored the workload of teachers and took effective action to support them in managing their work. They intervened when there was evidence that a teacher's workload was unrealistic, especially in the case of newly qualified teachers who, in their desire to involve themselves fully in the life of the school, sometimes took on too much. A range of strategies helped teachers to undertake routine activities, such as marking work, writing reports, keeping records and planning for the medium and short term, as efficiently as possible. Schools had begun to implement plans to transfer responsibility for the 25 tasks identified in the national workload agreement to reduce further the demands on teachers. The majority had taken*

steps to cut the amount of time spent in meetings by adopting more efficient procedures for conducting them; they insisted that they started and finished on time, had clear agendas that were followed closely, and that brief minutes were taken and circulated quickly. These changes often led not only to a reduction in workload, but also to an improvement in the quality of the activities.

(Ofsted, 2004, p. 4)

The wellbeing and workload of all who are employed in the school is important. Organizational stress is often related to the quality of leadership and management. Ineffective management generates stress and additional workload not only for teachers and other staff, but also for school managers themselves. So, what can be done?

WHAT CAN BE DONE?

We have noted earlier the importance of recruiting and retaining staff and the key role that a focus on wellbeing can play in both ensuring staff remain in teaching and are enabled to undertake a professionally fulfilling and satisfying job. For a deputy head involved in the ATL self-audit (see Chapter 4) participation in the project appeared to confirm a feeling that his job was impossible:

One of my action plans from the initial survey was to consider changing jobs. One of the options I considered was to leave teaching. This is still there. The balance remains 50:50 as to whether I stay or seek employment elsewhere. Some nights I am sick, have headaches and am irrationally unfair with my partner. A lot of that I put down to the pressures of my work. Other days I feel fulfilled and rewarded by what I do. It is the balance of these days that will determine my future.

(Bubb et al., 2003, p. 10)

Problems of stress can be tackled from both the individual level (see Chapter 5) and the level of the organization, with each making important contributions. Neither strategy on its own is likely to be successful. There are a variety of ways in which school leaders and managers can act positively to help reduce the possibility of stress. Brown and Ralph (1995) suggest that they should:

- help to de-stigmatize the idea of stress by putting it on the agenda for debate

- encourage the establishment of self-help groups to explore ways of solving problems

- develop an empathetic ethos or culture and offer support for self-help management techniques

- identify and liaise with people who can help

- draw up a school action plan after consultation to consider such factors as workload, resources, discipline, relationships, environment, career progression

- provide appropriate staff development

- make available information about counselling services and encourage staff to use them where necessary.

To this list we would add the need to give serious consideration to the Well-Being Programme (see Chapter 2).

Headteachers and other school leaders have a key role to play in ensuring that they effectively manage and lead their schools, but who is concerned with their welfare and wellbeing? It is becoming increasingly difficult to recruit headteachers – and not only to challenging schools – and one of the reasons suggested for this situation is that the job has become increasingly difficult to do (Earley, 2004; Hartle and Thomas, 2003) – is it simply a job too far? Is it also the case that heads are insufficiently supported in their work? Where, for example, do heads go for their support and how do they break down the loneliness that is experienced by being at the top of the organizational apex? We know from research for example that heads draw on a variety of sources, including governors, LEAs, leadership teams and professional associations, but it is their fellow headteachers who play the most significant role (Earley and Weindling, 2004).

Currently there is no shortage of training and professional development opportunities for school leaders and managers. These are available from a variety of sources including local education authorities, professional associations, higher education institutions and the NCSL. The latter, for example, through its national programmes, offers a number of opportunities for both middle and senior leaders. (A useful overview of current leadership and management programmes and other training and development opportunities is found in Earley and Bubb, 2004.) There is also no shortage of advice and guidance found on the Internet, via such websites as the Teacher Support Network, the DfES and the NCSL or if, like us, you prefer to read books (how old-fashioned!) then both Gold and Evans (1998) and Jones (2004) are very useful and thoughtful guides to good practice. In the rest of this chapter we consider networking, managing meetings, working practices, delegation and time-savers.

Networks

School leaders have always made good use of networks and found them a valuable form of support when and where they exist. The LEA can facilitate these. In Warwickshire, for example, a range of networks are currently on offer with local patch meetings seen as an effective self-supporting network, with colleagues from different phases meeting to discuss common concerns and issues. Similarly, in Wiltshire a support network for clusters of small schools has been established, which provides opportunities to network with colleagues in similar schools and to share expertise and resources (Earley and Evans, 2002).

A case could be argued that every head needs an individual mentor or counsellor to share their concerns in a non-threatening and trusting manner. The NCSL's consultant leader programme is one means by which this could be achieved but some LEAs have made distinct efforts to approach this problem through establishing such things as formal and informal mentoring arrangements for new heads. Very few, however, have attempted directly to address issues of wellbeing and work-life balance. Warwickshire LEA, for example, provides a free health check for its employees and, like a growing number of LEAs, is concerned about issues to do with work-life balance and general wellbeing. It offers its heads a one-day workshop entitled 'Self First for a Change'.

Another interesting example of how heads' concerns are addressed, taken from a LEA good practice guide to leadership development published by NCSL (Earley and Evans, 2002), can be found in Wiltshire LEA. This has been reproduced in Figure 8.2. Although these initiatives are about maintaining and enhancing the performance and motivation of headteachers, they were asked how the LEA could help to support them in reducing stress, managing time better and providing for their overall wellbeing. These are clearly key issues and the future of the leadership of our schools depends on them being adequately addressed.

Figure 8.2	Tackling the concerns of heads: examples from an LEA

In Wiltshire two initiatives are attempting to tackle the concerns of heads:

'Peer counselling for heads' was a small-scale pilot research project involving about eight primary headteachers who met for a day's training to consider such matters as peer counselling, how it relates to self-esteem, good communication, constructive feedback, and building peer support. This one-day conference was followed by the heads pairing up, visiting each other's schools, and then meeting a term later to evaluate and write up their findings. The heads spoke positively of the experience.

'Pastoral support for heads' was a related research project on how to ensure primary heads remained enthusiastic. Heads were carefully selected for this initiative. To participate they had to be successful heads who had been in post for five years or more, and of schools with 200 pupils plus and, crucially, to have managed to maintain their enthusiasm for the job. The programme consisted of four half-day sessions. Heads formed pairs but they could not be from the same area. Each pair had to share a success, 'walk' their schools and discuss with each other what it was that helps them to maintain their enthusiasm and motivation for the job. The whole group met at the end of the year to evaluate the value of the experience and write up their findings. They were asked how the LEA could help to support heads in reducing stress, managing time better and providing for their overall wellbeing.

Source: Earley and Evans, 2002.

Managing meetings

Managing meetings effectively is crucial because meetings can take up a great deal of school leaders' (and teachers') time, and some are notorious wasters of time. We have all sat through meetings that do not seem to have clear aims, or focused discussion, and time is wasted by repetition, or irrelevant comment. Decisions too often do not get made at such meetings, or, if they are, they are frequently rushed through with too little real consideration, with the result that they are likely to be implemented superficially. Another common problem is the meeting where one or two people dominate the proceedings, keeping the others out of the discussion at any significant level, and making them wonder why they are there at all.

The eventual outcome in both cases is that people become passive attenders – if, indeed, they attend at all. They place low priority on a system which apparently ignores their contribution, or values their time so little that it keeps them captive while others hold forth at unnecessary length. The net result of poor meetings is low-quality decision-making, followed by indifferent implementation of these decisions, for which there has been little ownership.

It is useful to identify the purpose of a meeting, and to ensure that everyone knows why they are there, and what part they are expected to play. At a briefing meeting, for example, participants would be expected to come unprepared, receiving information relatively passively. At a problem-solving meeting, on the other hand, members are most productive if they have thought about the issue under discussion, and are treated in such a way that they can participate fully. Many meetings have mixed functions, and it is helpful if the agenda – or Chair – makes it clear which items are which. Here are some things to consider, which are based on Shaw et al. (1992).

Calling the meeting:

- Is it necessary, or is it habit? What would happen if this meeting was not held?
- What do you want to achieve by this meeting?
- Who is needed? Are all of these people needed all of the time?
- Who is going to chair it?

Setting the agenda:

- What needs to be on it?
- What order of priority should they be in?
- Do some items need to be timed?
- Is the time allocation realistic?
- Is it clear who is responsible for each item?
- Are the start and end time clear?

Anticipating the meeting:

- Has everyone who is speaking to an agenda item been briefed?
- How will decisions be made?

- Who will take minutes? How will they be recorded (e.g. 'action minutes' to show who will do what and when)?

- Who or what is likely to be a problem at this meeting? Is there anything that can be done in advance to minimize the problem?

- How will AOB (any other business) be organized?

- What else can be done to ensure that the meeting wastes as little time as possible?

Good chairing skills include:

- starting and ending on time: formally opening and closing the meeting

- reminding of purpose, and ways of achieving it

- attending to timing of agenda items

- careful listening, paraphrasing, summarizing, understanding and analysing

- encouraging discussion through the Chair and ensuring 'fair play': everyone who wishes to contribute should be able to, the dominant may need silencing

- clarifying the protocols and setting a good standard of behaviour – dealing with interruptions, mobile phones, lateness

- careful reaching of consensus

- being courteous, thanking participants.

Working practices

All the time management issues in Chapter 5 are clearly relevant to school leaders but this group is expected and needs to be even more efficient in its working practices. There are many ideas for this in books and on websites such as the Teacher Support Network. The list below feels like teaching grandmothers to suck eggs but perhaps they'll serve as a useful reminder of what should be done.

- Invest time in setting up time-saving systems, such as a good filing system, templates for standard letters and procedures for routine tasks. Use time management tools and software: a diary, a to-do list, and a planner for long-term projects.

- Invest time into making yourself a healthy working environment – seating that doesn't hurt your back, computer positioning and lighting that doesn't result in eye strain and headaches.

- Schedule your activities, deciding how much time to devote to each task and setting realistic deadlines; set interim deadlines for major projects. Recognize what times of day best suit different activities.

- Make a daily to-do list and prioritize so that you tackle one thing at a time.

- Analyse your time use: review how much time you wasted on unimportant matters and tasks you should have delegated.

- Deal with new information effectively: act on it, delegate it, file it or throw it away.

- Give clear instructions: ask others to provide exactly what you need, in a form that suits you when you need it.

- Avoid overloading yourself: get involved only if you need to, ignore unnecessary detail, and delegate routine tasks.

- Minimize distractions: get an answerphone; only look at emails at set times and turn the volume on your computer down so that you don't know when someone has sent you an email; refuse unscheduled or unnecessary visits and meetings; and clear office clutter.

- Where do you work best? Maybe some tasks such as writing a bid or a report are hard to get done at school.

Avoiding procrastination or dithering is especially important for school leaders, as is dealing with interruptions.

Interruptions

Interruptions are commonly given as reasons for schedules being upset and things not getting done. But in a job like teaching or managing, where our business is dealing with people, interruptions are a necessary part of our work. However, we need to find ways of controlling interruptions so that they are more manageable. We need not be helpless victims of other peoples' interruptions. There are ways of handling interruptions that give us more control over our own time without making others feel as though they have been marginalized. A basic rule is to be attentive to people while they are with us, focusing on what they have to say, but to contain the visit/interruption to the shortest possible time. So, be courteous to people, but ruthless with time and get back on track at once.

There are ways of handling interruptions that give us more control over our time. The following list (based on Shaw et al., 1992) may be useful to you.

Keep interruptions as short as possible:

- Help the interrupter to keep to the point – don't get sidetracked into small talk.

- Explain that you're in the middle of something.

- Arrange to meet at a specified time later: after school may be too open-ended, unless a lot of time is needed; ten minutes before a lesson-bell limits the time and focuses the discussion.

- Remain standing – don't settle down comfortably.

- When summoned to consult, meet in neutral territory, or other person's: it's easier for you to leave.

- Use non-verbal signals to give hints: stand up, move towards door, glance at watch.

Consider the interrupter's needs:

- Give them your undivided attention.

- Don't interrupt, but get them to the point.

- Don't let your mind wander: it wastes time.

- Demonstrate that you have understood what is being said by paraphrasing the essence, thus focusing on the issue.

- Ensure, within reason, that they go away satisfied, perhaps with the promise of looking into it later, meeting again later, suggesting alternative support, even 'put it in writing' if necessary, but …

- Be assertive in saying 'no' if they are asking too much.

- Don't use interruptions as an excuse to procrastinate.

Procrastination

Sometimes we waste time procrastinating, avoiding tasks or distracting ourselves rather than getting on with the job. In order to assess yourself as a procrastinator, perhaps you might like to try out the quiz in Table 8.5 that one of us has used on management training courses (Shaw et al., 1992). Score yourself out of four depending on how strongly you think these statements apply to you.

Ways to stop procrastinating might include:

- being aware that you're procrastinating

- breaking large tasks into smaller ones

- giving yourself rewards

- tackling the unpleasant things first to get them out of the way

- considering the effects of NOT doing it

- using the 'one-hour' rule, i.e. deciding not to get up from the desk for one hour, but then have a short break.

Table 8.5	Are you a procrastinator? (Shaw et al., 1992)

Do you strongly agree = 4; mildly agree = 3; mildly disagree = 2; strongly disagree = 1	*Score*
1. I can always find a reason for not tackling a task I don't want to do.	
2. I need an imminent deadline before I get on with such a task.	
3. I put off tackling people if I think it's going to be unpleasant.	
4. There are too many interruptions and crises at school to allow me to accomplish anything that takes sustained effort.	
5. I like to tidy everything up before I get to grips with a task.	
6. When I know an unpopular decision has to be made, I tend to sit on the fence.	
7. I try to get other people to do the parts of my job that I don't like doing.	
8. My non-contact and 'management' time are rarely used for preparation or planning.	
9. I am under too much pressure to deal with difficult tasks.	
10. I often neglect to follow up what has been decided at a meeting.	
Total	

Procrastination quotient scoring:

0–20:   you are not a procrastinator.

21–30: although it is not a major problem, you do tend to put off tasks; paying some attention to this area should help you improve your time management.

30+: you have significant problems in procrastinating, and need to explore this further if you are to manage your time better.

◼ Delegation

Delegation has long been seen as an important management skill not only for survival but also to aid the development of others. In the current climate where distributed and shared leadership is the order of the day (see Earley and Weindling, 2004), effective delegation is more important than ever. Advice as to good practice is readily available and we have reproduced in Figure 8.3 that offered by the Teacher Support Network.

Figure 8.3	Effective delegation

Effective delegation – some ideas

1. Review the task, objectives, and deadline; consider whether it is part of a broader role or set of recurring tasks you wish to delegate.

2. Aim to delegate a complete activity, which will motivate a staff member and produce job satisfaction when successfully executed.

3. Assess the skills, knowledge, resources, influence and any other requirements for the task.

4. Consider the strengths, weaknesses, aspirations and existing workload of staff; choose the staff member to delegate to.

5. Identify the benefits for that person: for example, learning new skills, added variety in the workload or a step in career progression.

6. Assess the drawbacks of delegating the task: for example, the time you will need to commit to handing over and supporting the task, and the risk of failure.

7. Sell the benefits of undertaking the task to the person, explain the objectives and specify your requirements; address any concerns.

8. Agree the extent to which you will be involved, and clarify where responsibility lies; note that you retain ultimate responsibility.

9. Agree the schedule and deadlines; clarify to what extent, if any, you will need to review work in progress or be involved in decisions.

10. Provide any support and resources the staff member requires, such as training or access to information.

11. Inform other relevant staff; explain that the person will be acting on your authority and solicit their cooperation.

12. Liaise as the task progresses; encourage the person to approach you with any problems, but avoid unwanted interference.

13. Review the completed task; assess what the staff member has learnt, and any weaknesses that have been highlighted and should be tackled.

14. Review how effective your delegation skills were; identify and improve your contribution to any problems (e.g. poor communication or support).

Source: TSN website, accessed 2004.

◼ Time-savers

There is no shortage of ideas and suggestions for saving time and we outline just a few below taken from various websites. The National Remodelling Team gives several examples and mini case studies, including producing standard letters on line at David Lister secondary school in Hull. The school has 130 standard letters filed centrally, so teaching staff can find the letter template they need without having to rewrite it all over again. Staff choose a letter and email the Staff Support Team with the letter code and the names of the pupils whose parents they wish to send letters to. The team then mail-merge the letter with the school roll and send out hard copy letters to parents.

There are many areas of school activity which are perceived as bureaucracy concerns or 'bureaucratic burdens'. The main ones were outlined by the Implementation Review Unit (see Chapter 2) but where should schools start?

Find out what paperwork people consider is unnecessary, overly time-consuming or not useful. What alternatives are there? When deciding what to tackle first you could start with a relatively straightforward area of activity where you think you will be able to demonstrate 'quick wins', i.e., significant reductions in bureaucracy with little effort and expense. This will help staff, and governors, 'buy in' to investigating other areas. Or start with a project you are interested in. Enthusiasm is very useful. Consider the time of year. Does it make sense to start now?

The NRT website also gives an example of how heads' workload servicing governing bodies was reduced by working with governors to analyse the time spent in providing information and having meetings. Current practice can be audited and an action plan produced to make the governing body more efficient and reduce the head's workload. This may include setting a time limit for meetings, a limit to head's reports, reducing the number of governor committees and meetings with the Chair, and less involvement of governors in appointments, etc.

Schools spend a lot of time and money on recruitment. Identifying and offering jobs to people when they're on teaching practice can save a lot of time recruiting newly qualified teachers. The head of Penketh High School in Warrington sat in on the interviews for a head of maths at another school because he knew he would have a vacancy coming up. He invited two of the unsuccessful candidates to apply for his school's post.

Perhaps when a deputy or assistant headteacher leaves, consideration could be given to replacing them with a business manager or director of finance responsible for site facilities, finance, health and safety, and support staff management. Good business managers can save more money than it costs to employ them – potentially enabling more resources to be devoted to teaching and learning (see Chapter 7).

Communicating

Finally, communication is always a difficult issue in schools – how are staff kept informed of developments without overloading them with unnecessary detail? School leaders are often in a 'no-win' situation when it comes to communication – staff in the same school may complain about being kept in the dark, whilst others are concerned about getting too much information that is not directly related to them and their role in school!

We're sure you aim for open, honest two-way communication and make yourself available, encourage staff to raise problems and suggestions, and listen. But some communications need to be planned: think about your objectives and break down your message into a small number of key points. Anticipate your audience's attitude, current knowledge and level of interest; choose a time when they are likely to be receptive. Choose the right medium: for example, the phone for a quick discussion, and memos for complex information or where you need a written record. Communication is important and it is worth giving it careful consideration.

CONCLUSION

We conclude this chapter by reiterating a central theme that has been made throughout this book; that the effective leadership and management of staff – all staff, teachers and support staff – are critical to school improvement. We have seen that the roles of teaching and support staff are undergoing significant change as a result of current government policy and this has implications for school leaders. We stated in the first chapter that staff are the key resource in a school and it is through them that a school can improve its performance and be cost-effective. Staff are the most expensive resource in the budget of any school and it is therefore crucially important that they are enabled to work to the best of their abilities. It is here that 'human resource' matters, especially workload, well-being, morale, motivation and job satisfaction, and training and development come to the fore. The quality of leadership and management has been shown to be a key factor concerning staff retention.

No school can be said to be well led and managed, unless its most expensive and valuable resource, the staff, are deployed and managed effectively. Staff prefer managers who spend time getting to know them and who support them in their work. They usually like to be consulted and listened to, they respond to sensitive managers who communicate clearly and encourage debate, who make decisions, are positive, considerate and fair, and who lead by example. They perform better when they enjoy work, feel relaxed (or stress-free), their efforts are recognized and praise given, and they are seen as valuable individuals with skills (Evans, 1999).

'Looking after' staff and the strategies that can be used to enhance their wellbeing and make their workload manageable have been a central focus of this book. Without them the seven-point plan which forms the basis of the national agreement to tackle workload and raise standards will have less likelihood of success. However, we are optimistic about the future and see that there is now a real opportunity for schools to become the 'good employers' they should – and need – to be!

Appendix: websites

Association of Teachers and Lecturers: www.askatl.org.uk
General and Municipal Workers Union: www.gbm.org.uk
Hamilton Trust: www.hamilton-trust.org.uk
Health and Safety Executive: www.hse.gov.uk
Healthy Schools initiative: www.wiredforhealth.gov.uk
Higher level teaching assistants: www.hlta.gov.uk
Implementation Review Unit: www.dfes.gov.uk/iru
Learning and Skills Council: www.lsc.gov.uk
National Association of Head Teachers: www.naht.org.uk
National Association of Schoolmasters/Union of Women Teachers:
    www.teachersunion.org.uk
National College for School Leadership: www.ncsl.org.uk
National Employers' Organisation for Schoolteachers: www.lg-employers.gov.uk
National Remodelling Team: www.remodelling.org.uk
National Union of Teachers: www.teachers.org.uk
Professional Association of Teachers: www.pat.org.uk
Secondary Headteachers Association: www.sha.org.uk
Teacher Support Network: www.teachersupport.info
Teacher Training Agency: www.tta.gov.uk
Teachernet: www.teachernet.gov.uk/wholeschool/remodelling
Times Education Supplement: www.tes.co.uk
Unison: www.unison.org.uk/education

References

Association of Teachers and Lecturers (ATL) (2004) 'Independent schools ruining the home life of their teachers', press release, 5 April, London: ATL.

Audit Commission (2002) *Recruitment and Retention: A Public Service Workforce for the Twenty-First Century*, London, Audit Commission.

Blandford, S. (1999) *Managing Professional Development in Schools*, London: RoutledgeFalmer.

British Broadcasting Corporation (BBC) (2003) Head teacher defends Ascot trip, *BBC News*, 20 June.

Brown, M. and Ralph, S. (1995) 'The identification and management of teacher stress', in J. Bell and B. Harrison (eds), *Visions and Values in Managing Education*, London; David Fulton, pp. 195–205.

Bubb, S. (2003) *A Newly Qualified Teacher's Manual: How to Meet the Induction Standards*, 2nd edition, London: David Fulton.

Bubb, S. (2004a) *The Insider's Guide to Early Professional Development: Succeed in your First Five Years*, London: TES/RoutledgeFalmer.

Bubb, S. (2004b) 'Plagiarism is the classroom curse', *Times Educational Supplement*, 30 January, Jobs 1, p. 2.

Bubb, S., Earley, P. and Laverdure, A. (2003) *The ATL Teachers' Worktime Self-Audit Toolkit*, London: ATL and IoE.

Busher, H. and Harris, A. with Wise, C. (2000) *Subject Leadership and School Improvement*, London: Paul Chapman Publishing.

Chartered Institute of Personnel and Development (CIPD) (2001) *Married to the Job*, London: CIPD.

Chartered Institute of Personnel and Development (CIPD) (2003) *Living to Work?* London: CIPD.

Clarke, S. (1998) *Unlocking Formative Assessment*, London: Hodder & Stoughton.

Craven, J. (2003) 'Life blighted by named bananas and lice', *Times Educational Supplement*, 7 February.

Department for Education and Employment (DfEE) (2000a) *Supporting the Teacher Assistant: A Good Practice Guide*, London: DfEE.

Department for Education and Employment (DfEE) (2000b) *Teacher Assistant File: Induction Training for Teaching Assistants*, London: DfEE.

Department for Education and Skills (DfES) (2002a) *Time for Standards: Reforming the School Workforce*, London: DfES.

Department for Education and Skills (DfES) (2002b) *Developing the Role of School Support Staff*, London: DfES.

Department for Education and Skills (DfES) (2002c) *Looking for a Bursar?* London: DfES.

Department for Education and Skills (DfES) (2003a) *Raising Standards and Tackling Workload: A National Agreement*, London: DfES.

Department for Education and Skills (DfES) (2003b) *School Workforce in England*, London: DfES.

Dunham, J. (1995) *Effective School Management*, London: Routledge.

Earley, P. (2004) 'Attracting the next generation of school leaders: concerns and challenges', paper presented at the NW Belmas/SMEI symposium, Dublin, January.

Earley, P. and Bubb, S. (2004) *Leading and Managing CPD: Developing People, Developing Schools*, London: Sage/Paul Chapman Publishing.

Earley, P. and Evans, J. (2002) *LEAding Provision: School Leadership Development in LEAs: A Good Practice Guide*, Nottingham: NCSL.

Earley, P. and Weindling, D. (2004) *Understanding School Leadership*, London: Paul Chapman Publishing/Sage.

Edmonds, S., Sharp, C. and Benfield, P. (2002) *Recruitment to and Retention on Initial Teacher Training: A Systematic Review*, Slough: NFER.

Evans, L. (1999) *Managing to Motivate: A Guide for School Leaders*, London: Cassell.

Finlayson, M. (2002) Improving the wellbeing of teachers in Scotland, available on www.teachersupport.info/index.cfm?p=2250, accessed April 2004.

Fullan, M. (1991) *The New Meaning of Educational Change* (3rd edition, 2001), London: RoutledgeFalmer.

Fullan, M. (1993) *Change Forces: Probing the Depths of Educational Reform*, New York: Falmer Press.

Fullan, M. (2001) *Leading in a Culture of Change*, San Francisco: Jossey-Bass.

Fullan, M. (2003) 'We need lots of leaders', *Times Educational Supplement*, 11 July.

Gold, A. and Evans, J. (1998) *Reflecting on School Management*, London: RoutledgeFalmer.

Gold, A., Evans, J., Earley, P., Halpin, D. and Collarbone, P. (2003) 'Principled principals? Values-driven leadership: evidence from ten case studies of "outstanding" school leaders', *Education Management and Administration*, vol. 31, no. 2, pp. 125–36.

Haigh, G. (2004) 'Passing the big ten test', *Times Educational Supplement*, 9 April.

Hartle, F. and Thomas, K. (2003) *Growing Tomorrow's School Leaders: The Challenge*, Notingham: NCSL.

Hopper, B. (2003) 'Staff well-being: something for everyone – with no strings attached', *Professional Development Today*, vol. 6, no. 3, pp. 41–8.

Horne, M. (2001) *Classroom Assistance: Why Teachers Must Transform Teaching*. London: Demos/National Union of Teachers.

Health and Safety Executive (HSE) (1995) *Tackling Work-Related Stress: A Guide for Employers*, London: HSE.

Health and Safety Executive (HSE) (2000) *The Scale of Occupational Stress*, London: HSE.

Health and Safety Executive (HSE) (2003) *Managing Work-Related Stress: A Guide for Managers and Teachers in Schools*, London: HSE.

Health Development Agency, Department of Health (DH)/DfES, (2002) *Staff Health and Wellbeing*, Wetherby: Health Development Agency.

Implementation Review Unit (IRU) (2003) *IRU – Interim Report, April–November 2003*, Nottingham: DfES.

Johnson, S., Garland, P., Coldron, J., Coldwell, M., Fathallah-Caillau, I., Finlayson, I., Garland, I., Greaves, M., Power, L., Stephenson, K. and Williams, J. (2004) *A Systematic Mapping Exercise to Show How Existing Qualifications Fit with the Proposed Career Progression Framework for School Support Staff*, DfES research report 518.

Jones, J. (2004) *Management Skills in Schools*, London: Sage/Paul Chapman Publishing.

Leach, E. (2001) 'Not even the loos are bog-standard', *Times Educational Supplement*, 7 September.

Leithwood, K. and Riehl, C. (2003) 'What we know about successful school leadership: a report by Division A of AERA', Nottingham: NCSL.

Lepkowska, D. (2004a) 'Absentee teachers cost £1m per day', *Times Educational Supplement*, 26 March.

Lepkowska, D. (2004b) 'Teachers are working less, but success is some way off remodelling', *Guardian/NRT*, 16 April.

Mansell, W. (2002) 'Time off to work out, rest and play', *Times Educational Supplement*, 18 October.

Marsh, S. (2004) 'Buddha's way is best if you want to combat stress', *The Times*, 8 April.

Martin, J. and Holt, A. (2002) *Joined-up Governance*, Ely: Adamson Books.

McGraw, B. (2001) 'Preparation and professional formation of teachers: Early years to university', keynote presentation to UCET Autumn Conference, 19 November, Market Bosworth, UK.

Morris, E. (2001) *Professionalism and Trust*, London: Social Market Foundation.

Morrison, K. (1998) *Management Theories of Educational Change*, London: Paul Chapman Publishing/Sage.

National Joint Council for Local Government Services (NJC) (2003) *School Support Staff – the Way Forward*, London: Employers' Organisation.

Office for Standards in Education (Ofsted) (2002) *HMCI Annual Report*, London: Ofsted.

Office for Standards in Education (Ofsted) (2002) *Recruitment and Retention of Teachers and Headteachers: Strategies adopted by LEAs*, London: Ofsted.

Office for Standards in Education (Ofsted) (2004) *Leadership and Management: Managing the School Workforce*, London: Ofsted, available on Ofsted website.

Open University (1997) *MA Study Guide 'Leadership and Management in Education'*, Milton Keynes: Open University.

Parkinson, J. (2004) 'Minister confronted over classroom wages', *BBC News Online*, 7 April.

PriceWaterhouseCoopers (PWC) (2001) *Teacher Workload Study Interim Report*, London: DfES.

PriceWaterhouseCoopers (PWC) (2002) *Northern Ireland Teachers Health and Wellbeing Survey 2001*. Belfast: DENI.

Redhead, B. (2004) 'Start with the core issues', *Times Educational Supplement*, 2 April.

Sergiovanni, T. (1994) *Building Community in Schools*, San Francisco: Jossey-Bass.

School Teachers' Review Body (STRB) (2002) *Special Review of Approaches to Reducing Teacher Workload*, HMSO: London.

School Teachers' Review Body (STRB) (2003) *Report on teachers' workloads survey*, HMSO: London.

Shaw, M., Siddell, T. and Turner, M. (1992) *Time Management for Teachers*, Oxford: Oxford Brookes University.

Smithers, A. and Robinson, P. (2001) *Teachers Leaving*, Liverpool: Centre for Educational and Employment Research.

Smithers, A. and Robinson, P. (2003) *Factors Affecting Teachers Decisions to Leave the Profession*, research report RR430, London: Department for Education and Skills.

Stewart, W. (2004) 'Agreement could cut jobs', *Times Educational Supplement*, 9 April.

Stoll, L., Fink, D. and Earl, L. (2003). *It's About Learning (and It's about Time), What's in it for Schools?* London: RoutledgeFalmer.

Teacher Training Agency (TTA) (2003) *Professional Standards for Higher Level Teaching Assistants*, London: TTA.

Teacher Support Network (TSN) (2002) *Coping with stress*, TSN: London.

The Education Network (TEN) (2002) *Government Proposals for Remodelling the School Workforce*, PB38, London: TEN.

Thomas, H., Brown, C., Butt, G., Fielding, A., Foster, J., Gunter, H., Lance, A., Potts, L., Powers, S., Rayner, S., Rutherford, D., Selwood, I. and Szwed, C. (2003) 'Modernising the school workforce: developing perspectives', paper presented to BERA conference, Edinburgh, September.

Thomas, H., Brown, C., Butt, G., Fielding, A., Foster, J., Gunter, H., Lance, A., Potts, L., Powers, S., Rayner, S., Rutherford, D., Selwood, I. and Szwed, C., (2004) *Transforming the School Workforce Pathfinder Evaluation Project*, research summary, RBX03-04, Nottingham: DfES.

Totterdell, M., Jones, C., Heilbronn, R. and Bubb, S. (2002) 'The role of induction in teacher recruitment and retention', in C.W. Day and D. van Veen (eds), *Educational Research in Europe Yearbook 2002*, Leuven-Apledoorn: Garant/EERA.

Willson, T. (2004) 'Managing the battle against stress', *Manager: The British Journal of Administrative Management*, March/April, pp. 20–21.

Index